XML

A Manager's Guide

Addison-Wesley Information Technology Series
Capers Jones, Series Editor

The information technology (IT) industry is in the public eye now more than ever before because of a number of major issues in which software technology and national policies are closely related. As the use of software expands, there is a continuing need for business and software professionals to stay current with the state of the art in software methodologies and technologies. The goal of the Addison-Wesley Information Technology Series is to cover any and all topics that affect the IT community: These books illustrate and explore how information technology can be aligned with business practices to achieve business goals and support business imperatives. Addison-Wesley has created this innovative series to empower you with the benefits of the industry experts' experience.

For more information point your browser to
http://www.awl.com/cseng/series/it/

Wayne Applehans, Alden Globe, and Greg Laugero, *Managing Knowledge: A Practical Web-Based Approach.* ISBN: 0-201-43315-X

Gregory C. Dennis and James R. Rubin, *Mission-Critical Java™ Project Management: Business Strategies, Applications, and Development.* ISBN: 0-201-32573-X

Kevin Dick, *XML: A Manager's Guide.* ISBN: 0-201-43335-4

Jill Dyché, *e-Data: Turning Data into Information with Data Warehousing.* ISBN: 0-201-65780-5

Capers Jones, *Software Assessments, Benchmarks, and Best Practices.* ISBN: 0-201-48542-7

Capers Jones, *The Year 2000 Software Problem: Quantifying the Costs and Assessing the Consequences.* ISBN: 0-201-30964-5

Ravi Kalakota and Marcia Robinson, *e-Business: Roadmap for Success.* ISBN: 0-201-60480-9

David Linthicum, *Enterprise Application Integration.* ISBN: 0-201-61583-5

Sergio Lozinsky, *Enterprise-Wide Software Solutions: Integration Strategies and Practices.* ISBN: 0-201-30971-8

Patrick O'Beirne, *Managing the Euro in Information Systems: Strategies for Successful Changeover.* ISBN: 0-201-60482-5

Mai-lan Tomsen, *Killer Content: Strategies for Web Content and E-Commerce.* ISBN: 0-201-65786-4

Bill Wiley, *Essential System Requirements: A Practical Guide to Event-Driven Methods.* ISBN: 0-201-61606-8

Bill Zoellick, *Web Engagement: Connecting to Customers in e-Business.* ISBN: 0-201-65766-X

XML

A Manager's Guide

Kevin Dick

ADDISON–WESLEY

Boston • San Francisco • New York • Toronto • Montreal
London • Munich • Paris • Madrid
Capetown • Sydney • Tokyo • Singapore • Mexico City

The publisher offers discounts on this book when ordered in quantity for special sales. For more information, please contact:

Pearson Education Corporate Sales Division
One Lake Street
Upper Saddle River, NJ 07458
(800) 382-3419
corpsales@pearsontechgroup.com

Visit AW on the Web: www.awl.com/cseng/

Library of Congress Cataloging in Publication Data
Dick, Kevin, 1969–
        XML : a manager's guide / Kevin Dick.
            p.   cm.
        Includes bibliographical references (p.   ).
        ISBN 0-201-43335-4
            1. XML (Document markup language)   I. Title.
        QA76.76.H94D534   1999
        005.7'2—dc21   99-41252
                                                                CIP

ISBN 0-201-43335-4

Text printed on recycled and acid-free paper.
3 4 5 6 — MA — 03 02 01 00

Third Printing, June 2000

For my wife, Jane. I couldn't accomplish anything meaningful without your encouragement, perspective, and humor to support me.

Table of Contents

1.

The Internet Crisis: Exchanging Information

2.

XML Basics

3.
Related Standards

4.
XML Tools

5.
Processes and People

6.
Five XML Applications for Enterprises

7.

Five XML Applications for Vendors

Foreword

DAVID A. TAYLOR, PH.D.

The world turns faster than it used to. As recently as a decade ago, you could afford to ignore new technologies for a few years and let them mature. If they proved themselves in the market, they earned your attention. Now time is measured in Internet years, and new technologies can become standards before you even recognize their names.

So it is with XML. If you think XML is just for techies, or aren't sure what it is, you're already behind the curve. XML—the Extensible Markup Language—is the new standard for exchanging data electronically. It's brought to you by the same people who gave you the World Wide Web. Like the Web, it's about to transform your business.

At its simplest, XML is a better way of organizing Web content. But it' s so much more than that! Would you like to give your corporate customers machine-readable specs on all your products? XML is the right tool for the job. Want to accept and validate complex, multi-line orders over the Internet? XML will handle that, too. Need to integrate incompatible applications across your company? Combine information from inconsistent databases? Develop software that operates entirely over the Internet? XML will help you do all these things faster, better, and cheaper. This book will show you how.

XML is both elegant and deep. That poses a challenge; the elegance can quickly get lost in the depth. Like XML, this book is both elegant and deep. It conveys the essence of XML in a way that managers will easily understand and remember, then provides a practical guide to adoption. From its panoramic overview to its detailed roadmaps, the book both defines the territory and helps readers find their way within it.

An XML document arranges information in a hierarchy that allows readers—human and electronic—to understand the patterns in that information and to access it selectively. The document you hold in your hands does the same thing. From the executive briefings at the head of each chapter down to the fast-track summaries beside each paragraph, this book epitomizes structured access to information.

I take particular pleasure in the structure of this book because it is modeled after one of my own. I must have done something right; more than ten years after I wrote the first edition of *Object Technology: A Manager's Guide,* managers continue to buy it in bulk. Since that time, other authors have published books about technology with "Manager's Guide" in their titles. Some of these are fine books, but none of them so fully realizes the goals I set for the original manager's guide as does this one.

Preface

Purpose of This Book

Extensible Markup Language (XML) is an exciting new technology for exchanging structured information over **intranets, extranets**, and the **Internet**. As with many new software technologies, information flows into the developer community first. This flow starts electronically with e-mail lists, newsgroups, and technical Web sites. Then technology references, developer guides, and tutorials appear on bookstore shelves.

Technology information flows to developers first

After developers use a technology to create some inspiring prototypes, the computing press usually latches on to the trend. Articles hail it as the solution to a wide variety of application development problems. Executives take notice of the press coverage. They may even hear about internal **"skunkworks"** projects. Quickly, they want assessments of how the technology will affect their organizations.

Executives have access to high-level analysis

Managers get caught in the middle. They are at an *information disadvantage* when it comes to assessing the benefits of the technology and managing its use. On the one hand, developers are pushing from the bottom to use the technology on projects. On the other hand, executives are pushing from the top for formal technology planning. Unfortunately, information resources targeted specifically at managers are usually extremely limited. Therefore, managers must often resort to a time-consuming process of scanning volumes of developer-oriented details and dissecting executive summaries to synthesize a manager's perspective.

Managers are at an information disadvantage

This book addresses manager's information disadvantage with XML

XML: A Manager's Guide, addresses this problem for XML. It delivers:

❑ An introduction to XML technology and tools at a level that will allow managers to communicate with developers without having to become one.

❑ Information about the processes and people managers will need for successful XML projects.

❑ Inspiration for how to deliver value through XML, including an analysis of market adoption and the types of applications where it offers the most benefit.

Who Should Read This Book

This book targets managers working in IS and at software vendors

Obviously, this book targets managers. More specifically, it targets software development managers in (1) information systems (IS) organizations within enterprises and (2) product development groups within software vendors. To a great extent, the needs of these two different managerial audiences intersect. They both need a basic understanding of the technology as well as guidance in the tools, processes, and people necessary for success. They do differ in the types of XML applications relevant to their organizations, and this book accommodates the difference.

Different managers have different needs

Even within these two audiences, managers differ significantly in their individual backgrounds and managerial goals. Different managers will require different levels of detail for each of the three basic XML topics in the preceding list. To a certain extent, the level of detail required correlates with job responsibility. Table Preface-1 indicates how job responsibilities affect required level of detail.

This book accommodates different perspectives

As Table Preface-1 shows, technology planners and project managers will find this book most useful. Executives may find it useful to read portions of this book, but they will probably want to skip

Table Preface-1: Topics and audience

	Example IS Titles	Example Vendor Titles	Major Book Topics		
			XML Technology	Processes and People	Inspiration
Executive	CIO Director, IS	VP, Engineering VP, Marketing	Low detail	Low detail	Low detail
Technology Planning	Director, Technology Director, Architecture	CTO Product Manager	Medium detail	Medium detail	High detail
Project Management	Program Manager Project Manager	Director, Development Development Manager	Medium detail	High detail	Medium detail
Application Design	Systems Architect Systems Analyst	Chief Architect Technical Lead	High detail	Low detail	Medium detail

much of the detailed information. Application designers will find it a useful overview of XML technology and may find it provides some high-level inspiration. However, they will definitely want to acquire a more technical resource such as a developer's guide.

Organization of This Book

The organization of this book allows you to either read all the chapters sequentially or pick and choose the chapters that you find most interesting. All chapters after Chapter 1 begin with an Executive Summary section. After reading this section, you can decide whether you need the details provided in the rest of the chapter. You may also

You can read just parts of this book

quickly skim these details by using the Fast Track paragraph summaries, which appear in the margins. This book has seven chapters:

❑ **Chapter 1—The Internet Crisis: Exchanging Information.** Motivates the need for XML by examining the requirements left unfilled by existing Internet technologies.

❑ **Chapter 2—XML Basics.** Introduces fundamental XML concepts at a level that enables you to understand XML application without going into the details necessary for you to develop such applications. It has a Technical Summary section at the end that helps you refresh your memory about basic XML concepts.

❑ **Chapter 3—Related Standards.** Gives an overview of standards and emerging standards closely related to XML, including an analysis of their benefits and some simple example code. It also has a Technical Summary section at the end.

❑ **Chapter 4—XML Tools.** Analyzes the types of tools necessary to build applications that use XML and mentions some of the leading vendors of such tools.

❑ **Chapter 5—Processes and People.** Analyzes the software development processes and staff necessary to deploy XML applications. It uses three general application categories to abstract common process and staff requirements. You will probably want to concentrate on the category that matches the applications you plan to build.

❑ **Chapter 6—Five XML Applications for Enterprises.** Presents an architectural overview of five XML applications important for enterprises and discusses the benefits of using XML in these applications.

❑ **Chapter 7—Five XML Applications for Vendors.** Presents an architectural overview of five XML applications important for vendors of software products and services and discusses the benefits of using XML in these applications.

As you can see, the last three chapters focus on the needs of project managers, enterprise technology planners, and vendor technology planners, respectively. If you don't fall into the primary audience for one of these chapters, you may wish to read only the Executive Summary. Applying this advice to all chapters, Table Preface-2 suggests which parts of which chapters each target audience should read.

Chapters 5 through 7 have specific audiences

There is a Glossary at the end of the book that defines many of the XML and general Internet terms used in this book. You will find it helpful if you come across an unfamiliar term or simply want to refresh your memory of its definition. The first time a word defined in the Glossary appears, it is set in color. Terms specific to XML appear in italics, while general Internet terms appear in plain typeface.

Highlighted words appear in the Glossary

Table Preface-2: Suggested reading

	Executive	Technology Planning	Project Management	Application Design
Chapter 1	Entire	Entire	Entire	Entire
Chapter 2	Summary	Entire	Entire	Entire
Chapter 3	Summary	Entire	Summary	Entire
Chapter 4	Summary	Entire	Entire	Entire
Chapter 5	Summary	Entire	Entire	Summary
Chapter 6	Summary	Selected Sections	Entire	Selected Sections
Chapter 7	Summary	Selected sections	Summary	Selected sections

Acknowledgments

This book would not be possible without the patience and hard work of Mary O'Brien and the rest of the team at Addison-Wesley.

I'd like to thank my reviewers:

> Lauren Wood
>
> Mary LaPlante
>
> Liam Quin
>
> Alfie Kirkpatrick
>
> Dan Appelquist
>
> David A. Epstein
>
> Tim Kientzle

Special thanks to the following people, who thoughtfully reviewed two drafts:

> Eve Maler
>
> David A. Taylor, Ph.D.
>
> David Turner

Much gratitude to Dad, Mom, Adam, Goutam, Matt, Rafe, Todd, and Walter. Your many helpful suggestions on the manuscript and many software-related discussions over the years greatly contributed to the quality of this book.

1

The Internet Crisis: Exchanging Information

Connections Without Understanding

Without question, the Internet is a revolutionary phenomenon. In just five years, it completely transformed the landscapes of both personal and enterprise computing. The word processor used to be the most important application on a personal computer. Now it's the Web browser. The database used be the most important piece of software in an enterprise computing architecture. Now it's the Web application server. What makes the Internet so compelling?

The Internet is a revolutionary phenomenon

Connectivity Is the Key

The revolutionary benefit of the Internet is *connectivity*. It's easy to get a connection. Having a connection provides access to a broad range of resources. From a technical standpoint, the Internet is a networking protocol, **TCP/IP**, with a suite of application protocols running on top of it, for example, **FTP**, **HTTP**, and **SMTP**. These protocols are all standardized. Standardization results in easy connectivity. Anyone can connect a computer running standard application protocols to the Internet using standard networking hardware and, all of sudden, everyone else can access information stored on that computer.

The Internet delivers standardized connectivity

This easy connectivity has convinced a very large number of people and organizations to connect themselves using the standard Internet protocols because it creates a positive feedback loop. As more people and resources become connected, the value of connecting additional people and resources becomes greater.

Connectivity breeds greater connectivity

The Internet connects all consumers to all services

If the only resource on the Internet were an online bookstore, a few prolific readers might invest the time and money necessary to get a connection. But the fact that people can buy books, music, and computer hardware—as well as look up information about companies, hobbies, and long-lost friends—makes hundreds of millions of people willing to connect themselves. The existence of all these users creates a market for even more products and services.

Intranets connect all employees to all systems

Similarly, if intranets provided enterprises only with the ability to connect all their employees to internal human resource applications, enterprises might invest a few million dollars in the technology. But the fact that intranets can connect all employees to all applications and databases in an enterprise—as well as connect these resources to customers and suppliers—makes enterprises willing to spend tens or hundreds of millions of dollars on intranets. Clearly, there is a snowball effect to the Internet.

Everything may be connected eventually

Some people believe that Internet connectivity will snowball to the point where virtually everything containing a computer chip is connected. For example, sensors in your car's fuel pump could detect a problem, send a message to the car's central computer, which would then inform the computer at your repair shop. The repair shop's computer would automatically order new parts from the manufacturer. The car's central computer would query your electronic datebook for a good time to visit the repair shop, enter the appointment, and inform you via a screen on the dashboard. Don't worry about forgetting your appointment. Your electronic datebook would automatically page you.

Unfulfilled Requirements

Traditional Internet technology is inadequate

Unfortunately, there is a challenge to this universal connectivity. To illustrate the challenge, consider the following tasks, which should be easy but are in fact difficult with traditional Internet technology.

❏ **Customized page layout.** There are many times when you might want to customize the layout of a Web page when you access it. Perhaps you have poor eyesight and want larger fonts. Perhaps you're accessing the page from a small device such as a cellular phone and want to format it for the smaller display. Perhaps you want to filter the Web page to display only recent information. With traditional technology, the Web page author must provide completely different pages to support each mode of access.

❏ **Downloadable product comparisons.** One of the great things about the Web is that there is a wealth of information about the features and prices of products and services. The availability of this information makes comparison shopping very efficient and many providers have emerged to deliver this service. But suppose you use one of these services to construct a comparison matrix and want to import it into a spreadsheet so that you can add your own information. With traditional technology, you might have to cut and paste each cell of the table manually into the spreadsheet.

❏ **Application integration.** The Internet makes it possible for enterprises to connect different business applications physically for processes such as accounting, human resources management, and manufacturing resource planning. Unfortunately, these applications cannot understand each other's data formats unless the enterprise develops expensive custom translation software.

❏ **Data integration.** As organizations have evolved over time, they have accumulated scores of different databases to support different business processes. Together, these databases represent a valuable resource. The Internet makes it possible to unify access to these resources physically, but each resource often has its own way of representing data, making it difficult to present a set of coherent, business-oriented views of the data to end users.

❏ **Interchangeable files.** Connecting everyone to the Internet naturally motivates people to try to share the information they've created. You've probably experienced the frustration of attempting such a file transfer only to discover that your audience can't read the file format you used. This problem is particularly frustrating in software development. Developers tend to have different preferences in the particular tools they like to use. Moreover, a given development project will often employ a variety of different types of tools. Getting all these tools to exchange files seamlessly is so difficult that most organizations force developers to use the same tools and restrict the types of tools used in the organization. These measures hurt developer productivity.

XML can solve these problems

Whereas traditional Internet technologies have difficulty accommodating these tasks, Extensible Markup Language (XML) does not. XML makes it easier for different people and different pieces of software to understand information exchanged over the Internet.

Roots of the Connection Problem

The problem is different perspectives

Understanding how XML can help you overcome the challenges of universal connectivity begins with analyzing the root cause of the problem. The underlying issue is that each party that accesses a piece of information has its own perspective on what that information means. The more parties that become linked, the greater the opportunity for misunderstanding.

Spoken language illustrates the problem of different perspectives

Consider the case of spoken language. You probably find it easy to communicate with your immediate family and coworkers. Now expand the number of people with whom you communicate. As you expand outside your immediate geographical location, you will find people use different colloquialisms. As you expand outside your profession, you will find people use different jargon. If you expand the number of people with whom you communicate far enough, you will encounter completely different languages. The more people with whom you speak, the greater the opportunity for miscommunication.

Let's analyze a detailed example of different perspectives on the Internet. Suppose you plan to buy a CD-ROM drive on line. An easy enough task if you want to visit just one online store. But suppose you want to compare prices at several different Web sites selling computer hardware. Each Web site has a top-level page with the different categories of products it offers. The first site you visit has a "CD-ROM" category. The second one does not but it does have a "Storage Devices" category, which you find contains CD-ROM drives. The third one also has a Storage Devices category, but this category has only "Fixed," "Removable," and "Optical" subcategories. It turns out that CD-ROM drives are in the "Removable" subcategory. Yet a fourth site has a "Storage Devices" category with no CD-ROM drives. This particular site put them in the "Multimedia" category. Once you find a list of CD-ROM drives at each site, you face another problem. Some list them by product description and others by manufacturer serial number. How do you compare prices if you're not sure they apply to the same item?

Online stores categorize CD-ROM drives differently

You would probably surmount the obstacles to online comparison shopping for CD-ROMs given enough time, but what about an automated shopping agent? It should be easy to create a software program that visits each retail site and discovers the price for a particular product. Unfortunately, with different organizational and product listing schemes, the shopping agent will probably be unable to gather pricing information from every site, making it difficult to find the lowest price. People compensate for the Web's current shortcomings in representing information by spending more time in

Automated agents need standard formats

their searches. We are denied much of the Internet's potential for automatically gathering and processing information. Delivering on this potential is difficult with *ad hoc* information representation.

Enterprises need standard definitions of business concepts

The problem of automated information processing is particularly acute for enterprises. One of the great promises of Internet computing is connecting enterprises to their suppliers, partners, and customers so that they can achieve inventory, manufacturing, and distribution efficiency. However, it turns out that each company's information systems define common business concepts such as product, order, and invoice differently. Even within one company, different divisions often have different definitions of these business concepts. Imagine the differences that exist between different companies in different industries located in different parts of the world. How could an enterprise make its information systems cooperate with a foreign supplier? Solving the problem for one supplier is easy. Build a one-to-one translation program. Unfortunately, most enterprises deal with hundreds of suppliers, requiring the construction and maintenance of hundreds of translators. The resulting business environment is hardly a picture of free-flowing global electronic commerce.

Electronic commerce is only one example

In the preceding examples, the greater the connectivity, the more difficulty in achieving understanding among all parties. Although both examples are of electronic commerce applications, the problem of information exchange extends to all aspects of the Internet. Electronic commerce is simply an example where many people agree that billions of dollars are at stake.

Convergence of Information Exchange Problems

The problem of achieving understanding among many parties is endemic in all areas of distributed computing. People have developed many applications for distributed networks. As the reach of these networks has grown, these applications have encountered the information exchange problem. The heart of the problem is *spontaneity.* If people were able and willing to negotiate the format of messages with each new party for each application, there would be no problem. However, the cost in time and money of such an arrangement is prohibitive on any but the smallest scale. People want software that can spontaneously connect across the globe, exchange information, and then process that information. The convergence of information exchange problems in many different areas makes finding a solution extremely important. Any technology that helped solve the problem could expect rapid adoption in a wide variety of applications. There are several important areas where the problem is particularly acute.

Spontaneous information exchange is the problem

Web Documents

The number of documents accessible using the Web is staggering. Unfortunately, it's hard to figure out what any of the documents mean without actually reading them. Take search engines as an example. Suppose you wanted to find online versions of works by William Shakespeare. A search on "William Shakespeare" would return documents he has written, documents written about him, and documents describing people's preferred authors. In all probability, the number of documents in the latter two categories would be much greater than the number in the first. What's the problem? There is no agreement on how to indicate what a particular word or phrase means. Therefore, documents where William Shakespeare means "document author," "document subject," and "preferred

Undifferentiated text makes Web searches difficult

author list element" all look the same. Consequently, people are either unable to find what they need or it takes much longer than they want.

HTML is simply a page layout language

The problem lies with **HTML,** by far the most widely used means of delivering information over the Web. HTML is essentially an online page layout language. Authors can use it to place information in specific parts of the screen and control the format of information. HTML is an adequate page layout language. Web page authors have used it to create some very nice looking pages. However, it offers no way for those authors to provide any description of the information itself.

Data exchange is difficult with HTML

Another area of inadequacy for HTML is analyzing information. Suppose you use a Web-based home search service to develop a list of homes that meet your criteria. Once you have the list, you might want to analyze it in a number of different ways. You might want to sort by price. You might want to sort by square footage. You might want to group by school district. The Web site may be able to perform the transformations you want, but all the processing occurs on the Web server. It sends you formatted text. This approach limits you to the filtering options provided by the Web site and places a heavy processing load on the Web server, causing response delays. A more flexible and efficient approach would be to send the data itself to the browser and let a built-in spreadsheet give you the power to slice and dice the data any way you wished. Unfortunately, the Web server has no way to send the data to browsers in a format that it knows they can understand. Therefore, people do not have the ability to utilize fully the data they find and it takes more time than necessary to perform what analysis is possible.

Electronic Commerce

Electronic commerce is perhaps the best example of the information exchange problem. It is clear why parties previously unknown to each other want to exchange information, and there is an obvious monetary value to the exchange. There are two fundamental types of electronic commerce: business to consumer and business to business.

E-commerce includes business-to-consumer and business-to-business commerce

In business-to-consumer commerce, the information exchange problem imposes a time penalty. As discussed in the CD-ROM drive example, people can compensate for different information representations at different electronic commerce sites by manually developing knowledge of the site structure. This process requires time and eliminates the possibility of timesaving automated shopping agents. It also eliminates the possibility of higher level automated tasks. What if you wanted to find CD-ROM drives compatible with your existing **SCSI** controller card? This information is available at manufacturer sites. However, there is no standard way for you to describe the characteristics of your SCSI controller card or for manufacturers to describe compatibility information for their drives. This information is buried in paragraphs of text. So, you have to read every manufacturer's CD-ROM drive data sheet. The information exchange problem also makes it difficult to eliminate mundane tasks such as online product registration. You have to type in your name, address, phone number, e-mail, and other information for every product that you buy.

Time is the barrier in business-to-consumer commerce

In business-to-business commerce, the information exchange problem imposes money and choice penalties. If two businesses want to conduct electronic commerce, they have to agree beforehand on a message format. Developing the software code to implement such agreements costs money. Requiring prior agreement also restricts choices to companies with which an enterprise has prior agreements.

Money and choice are the barriers to business-to-business commerce

If an innovative new company comes along that offers substantially lower prices and higher quality, the enterprise is out of luck until it can reach an agreement on data format with this new party.

Database Access

Employees need a coherent view of data

As discussed earlier, enterprises have accumulated a lot of data in various databases over the years. The current problem is delivering it to people in a way that increases productivity. Certainly, it is easy for any one person to access any one database by installing the appropriate software on a client machine and executing queries against the database. However, in many cases, the information that a particular person needs to do a job resides in many different databases. Take the typical customer service representative as an example. The representative may need to help customers place orders, check on shipments, correct account information, configure products, and get replacement parts. Each of these tasks may require accessing a different database. In many cases, the representative simply cannot help customers with certain tasks. In others, it may be necessary to switch back and forth between different database access programs, writing notes on pieces of paper, to assemble the information necessary to assist the customer. This database Tower of Babel costs time and customer goodwill. There is a plethora of other examples of database access problems, including sales representatives trying to check manufacturing schedules for multiple products, marketing analysts trying to assemble historical sales information for multiple products, and executives trying to analyze sales trends across divisions.

Data access becomes harder with more user perspectives

The database access problem becomes even more acute as the enterprise expands the number of people who have access to the data. There is a trend toward empowering employees throughout the enterprise by giving them access to the information they need to make good decisions. But if they cannot process this information, it does not help them. Each employee has specific information requirements particular to his job tasks. Simply throwing data at the employee doesn't help. There is also a trend toward making corporate data available to strategic partners and even customers so that they can integrate their operations more fully with the enterprise. Of course, if the enterprise has trouble providing its own employees with the data they need, delivering it to outsiders is nearly impossible. For years, enterprises have searched for a technology that could help them synthesize data from different databases into different packages, depending on the needs of the particular user. Such a technology would help reduce costs as well as increase the capabilities to deliver innovative products and services.

Knowledge Sharing

With people tackling ever more complex problems, a fundamental barrier to innovation is cooperation among large groups. A major source of difficulty is effectively sharing knowledge of a complex topic. Consider three scenarios: a joint product development effort among five companies, a research partnership among twelve laboratories to create medicines based on gene sequencing, and joint combat exercises that include a dozen ships and a hundred aircraft from three different countries. All of these scenarios have a common problem. Individual participants want to share their knowledge with the rest of the group and integrate the group's knowledge into their understanding of the problem.

Inadequate knowledge sharing is a barrier to cooperation

Sharing the information itself is not too difficult. One approach is for each participant to do a presentation in a teleconference. However, this approach does not make it easy for a participant to integrate the knowledge shared by everyone else. Although presentation slides may be an effective means of organizing high-level concepts, they are not very useful for exchanging detailed information. The

Teleconferencing is adequate for high-level concepts

product development participants need the three-dimensional models of product concepts and specifications for different prototype parts. The research partnership participants need gene sequences and protein synthesis simulations. The joint naval exercise participants need detailed sensor deployment plans, rules of engagement contingencies, and weapon delivery assignments.

Combining high-level and low-level perspectives is a challenge

A further refinement of the presentation approach is to follow up with electronic versions of software files that contain the detailed information. There is the small problem of different participants using different file formats. There is the large problem of relating these files to the original presentation and to each other. Fundamentally, there is no way for one participant to create an information package that includes all the connections among different elements that make it truly meaningful. Such information packages along with standard file formats would accelerate the pace of innovation and enable the coordination of larger groups in real-time tasks.

Metadata Standard Is a First Step

Spontaneous information exchange requires metadata

The convergence of information exchange problems from different areas of distributed computing reveals the importance of a general-purpose approach for enabling spontaneous information exchanges. Such an approach would have to meet two requirements: (1) a party could indicate what each piece of information means and (2) two parties could spontaneously agree on the organization of information. The first step in developing such an approach is to meet requirement (1) by adding **metadata** to documents.

Metadata is data about data

Metadata is data about data. For instance, "author" is metadata about "William Shakespeare." A database schema comprises metadata about the data in the database—it gives all data in a column the same description, such as, "Customer Number," and indicates the datatype of data in that column, such as currency, integer, or string. A distributed object interface definition comprises metadata about the objects that implement that interface—it describes the behaviors an object implements and the arguments necessary to activate each behavior. Metadata is a formal way to describe what a piece of information means.

Metadata addresses requirement (1) for a general-purpose approach to spontaneous information exchange. However, it does not address requirement (2). Metadata by itself would allow the home search site mentioned previously to describe a set of search results as useful data. But the user's browser would not understand the organization of that description. If "Home Price" has the metadata "number" attached, what does that mean? What if the metadata were "numeric," "int," or "dollars"? Does the browser need a library of common terms for the same concept? Metadata alone certainly wouldn't solve the problem of business-to-business commerce. What if the metadata "price" attached to "100,000" meant U.S. dollars for one company and pounds sterling for the other? Metadata makes it easier to locate interesting data and associate a piece of data with a description, but it still requires the explicit agreement of each party. The parties have to agree on the structure of the metadata.

Metadata solves only half the problem

Shared Context Standards Deliver True Understanding

Shared context is a formal description of the rules metadata must follow. A shared context applies to a particular type of document and serves as a contract between the document sender and document receiver. The document sender agrees that the document

Shared context serves as a contract between parties

conforms to the shared context. The document receiver agrees to interpret the document according to the shared context.

Companies must agree on a shared context for commerce

In the case of business-to-business commerce, two companies may agree to a shared context for "Order" documents. Part of this shared context might be that (a) an "Order" can have one or more "Line items"; (b) each "Line item" has an "SKU," a "Unit Price," and a "Quantity"; and (c) "Unit Price" is a number with two decimal places and represents U.S. dollars. This approach helps address many of the information exchange problems just discussed.

❑ To solve the problem of organizing data on the Web such as home search results, one could develop a universal shared context for tabular data.

❑ One could help solve the database access problem by defining a universal shared context that describes how a database organizes data and the relationship of the data to common business concepts.

❑ Electronic commerce would become much more efficient through shared contexts for catalog structure, orders, and receipts.

❑ The knowledge sharing problem would become easier by defining a shared context for each class of problems that multiple parties want to solve jointly, for example, one for product development, one for developing medicines from gene sequences, and one for naval task force combat information.

People can publish shared contexts over the Internet

Shared context does not provide complete spontaneity, but it comes close. At least one party must develop the shared context. However, the party can then make the shared context available on the Internet and anyone else can participate in the information exchange it governs. The shared context developer doesn't even have to be a party to these exchanges. One could imagine an organization dedicated to developing such shared contexts as a community service or commercial venture. It might never even use the shared context itself; it would simply provide the seed for other parties to begin spontaneous information exchange. The beauty of this solution is that the connectivity of the Internet becomes part of the solution. The developer of a shared context can simply post it to the Internet, where it becomes available to anyone that is interested.

The XML Approach

The concepts of metadata and shared context are general ones. There are many different ways to implement them. XML is an increasingly popular implementation and will almost certainly be the most widely used. XML is an outgrowth of Standard Generalized Markup Language (SGML), which became a standard of the International Organization for Standardization (ISO) in 1986. SGML had its early origins in IBM, which wanted a means of describing document content so that it could publish the same content in a number of different ways. For instance, it would be nice to have the ability to deliver the same technical information about a new product feature as a stand-alone bulletin for existing users and as part of a user's guide for new users. Because other organizations were struggling with similar problems, it made sense to create a standard for document markup. The result of the standards process was a rich document markup language that allowed authors to separate the logical content of a document from its presentation. The fundamental approach was to add metadata to denote this logical structure and provide shared context for specifying the metadata rules followed by each type of document.

XML is a descendant of SGML

HTML is also a descendant of SGML. But it was never intended as a general means of defining metadata. It predefines a narrow set of

XML is optimized for the Internet

metadata specific to page layout. SGML and HTML leave the requirement for a standard means of defining metadata on the Internet unfulfilled. However, when people began to develop such a standard, they naturally looked to SGML as a starting point. The **World Wide Web Consortium (W3C)** formed a working group to study the issue in July 1996. The goal of this group was to produce a simplified subset of SGML suitable for use on the Web. Why a simplified version? SGML is extremely complex and poses some problems for automated processing of large volumes of Internet documents. It seemed that a subset of SGML could be simple enough for people to understand in its entirety, yet expressive enough to meet the need for shared context on Internet. The result was the XML 1.0 specification, released as a "recommendation," the highest level of W3C endorsement, on February 10, 1998.

Tags provide metadata, DTDs provide shared context

The XML approach to metadata and shared context is simple. Authors add metadata through **tags.** The syntax for adding these tags is very similar to that of HTML. To indicate that William Shakespeare is the author of a work, one could write "<author>William Shakespeare</author>." Document designers add shared context through *document type definitions* (DTDs). A **DTD** is a set of declarations that specify the allowable order, structure, and attributes of tags for a particular type of document. A document references the DTD that governs its structure, either inline or with an Internet uniform resource locator (URL). Therefore, any party can spontaneously access the DTD, interpret its rules, and process the document.

XML requires software support

For successful application of its approach to metadata and shared context, a wealth of different types of software must support XML. At the end of the day, software applications must be able to produce and process XML documents. There are five basic requirements for XML software support.

❑ **Fundamental software components.** These components provide low-level XML capabilities such as parsing and generating documents. Developers use these components to build XML-capable software. Wide availability of these building blocks from different vendors and for different programming languages is necessary to ensure wide availability of higher level XML software.

❑ **Software development tool support.** To embed XML capabilities in applications rapidly, developers need tools that have special features that improve productivity. These features go beyond the simple inclusion of fundamental software components. They include utilities for manipulating XML documents and integrating with document development tools.

❑ **Document development tools.** Obviously, people must be able to define DTDs and author XML documents. They need tools that make this process easier than using a text editor. They need graphical modeling tools for creating DTDs and hierarchical browsers for directly manipulating XML documents. They also need support from existing Web content development and management tools.

❑ **Web infrastructure support.** Although XML is useful for many different types of information exchange problems, it is a Web technology. To develop adoption momentum, Web infrastructure such as browsers and servers must support it. Availability of this infrastructure as part of the Internet will provide additional leverage for people trying to solve domain-specific information exchange problems. If developers know that anyone with a standard Web browser can view XML documents, they are much more likely to use XML.

❑ **Translation components.** Existing software applications already have their own data formats. To maintain compatibility with existing systems, they must still support these formats. But to integrate with other applications through XML they must support XML. The simplest solution is for these applications to use translation components to convert their data formats into XML. This process is analogous to word processors supporting the "Save As Rich Text Format" feature. To make this transition quickly, developers of these applications need components that provide the foundation for building these translation features.

The possibilities for XML may cause confusion

If XML achieves support in these types of software, its close relationship with existing Internet technologies will make it an extremely attractive solution to most information exchange problems. In some sense, the W3C greatly exceeded expectations. Not only did it develop a technology for solving the Web document information exchange problem, it developed a technology with the potential to solve information exchange problems in every area of distributed computing. Unfortunately, the generality of the solution poses a problem. Because the potential application of XML is so broad, there is opportunity for confusion. Groups trying to solve different information exchange problems with XML may conduct conflicting educational campaigns about the technology's benefits and make conflicting demands on tool vendors. It is important for individuals and organizations faced with information exchange problems to understand how XML can help them, the tools they need to deliver solutions, and how they can overcome the inevitable barriers to deployment.

2

XML Basics

Executive Summary

Understanding the mechanisms behind XML is crucial to understanding its potential and effectively managing development projects that use it. Going through the process of learning these mechanisms will help you develop the thought processes necessary to analyze the return on investment of using the technology on a particular project. Also, although you probably won't create XML documents themselves, a basic command of its syntax arms you with the information necessary to communicate effectively with developers.

You should understand how XML works

The XML specification itself has two parts, one for XML documents and one for XML DTDs. The document portion specifies how to use **tagged markup** to indicate the meaning of data. The DTD portion specifies how to indicate the allowable structure for a class of XML documents.

The XML standard covers documents and DTDs

Many people use the term "XML" to refer to a broader Internet document paradigm in which XML documents serve as the foundation. This paradigm includes related standards that add functionality such as hypertext links and page layout. Chapter 3 introduces several of these standards. This paradigm also includes domain-specific standards defined in terms of XML documents for such tasks as Web commerce and supply chain management. Chapters 6 and 7 include some brief descriptions of several domain standards. Figure 2-1 shows how XML supports this larger paradigm.

XML is part of a larger paradigm

As you can see, the paradigm is fully modular; you can choose which parts to use for any particular application. Some applications may use only XML documents. Others may include XML DTDs as well. Still others may take advantage of related standards or domain

Figure 2-1:
XML supporting a
larger paradigm

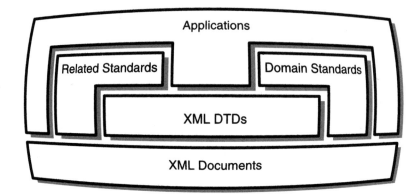

standards. It is very important when discussing the application of
XML to a particular problem to establish clearly which parts of the
paradigm you intend to use.

Jumping In

*We'll start with a
simple example*

A simple business card example illustrates the key technical features of XML. People spontaneously exchange physical business
cards every day. XML makes it very easy to do the same thing electronically. The document in Example 2-1a contains much of the
data found on a business card.

Example 2-1a

```
<business_card>
  <name>
    <given_name>Kevin</given_name>
    <middle_name>Stewart</middle_name>
    <family_name>Dick</family_name>
  </name>
  <title>Software Technology Analyst</title>
  <author/>
  <contact_methods>
    <phone>650-555-5000</phone>
```

```
    <phone>650-555-5001</phone>
   </contact_methods>
</business_card>
```

As you can see, tags in XML documents are similar to those in HTML documents. Familiar open and close tags define the beginning and end of *elements*. These elements appear in a strict hierarchy—"given_name" is a child of "name," which is a child of "business card." The most important difference from HTML is that you can define any types of elements you choose rather than relying on a predefined set.

XML tags are similar to HTML tags

DTDs describe the allowable structure of XML documents. A document does not have to have a DTD, but using a DTD is a convenient way for two parties to ensure that they are using the same data format. A DTD can constrain the pieces of data that may occur in a document, the hierarchy of data, and the number of times each piece of data may appear. Example 2-1b shows a DTD for our simplified business card document.

DTDs constrain document structure

Example 2-1b
```
<!ELEMENT business_card (name, title, author?, contact_methods)>

<!ELEMENT name (given_name, middle_name?, family_name)>
<!ELEMENT given_name (#PCDATA)>
<!ELEMENT middle_name (#PCDATA)>
<!ELEMENT family_name (#PCDATA)>

<!ELEMENT title (#PCDATA)>

<!ELEMENT author EMPTY>

<!ELEMENT contact_methods (phone*)>
<!ELEMENT phone (#PCDATA)>
```

DTDs describe the type and number of elements

A DTD lists the types of elements within a document, the types of child elements for these elements, and so on. Special characters such the "?" and the "*" constrain the number of times an element may appear, in this case 0 or 1 times and 0 or more times, respectively. So our DTD says that a business card may have 0 or 1 author elements, 0 or 1 "middle_name" elements, and 0 or more "phone" elements.

XML Conceptual Model

XML can support sophisticated documents

Our business card example is extremely simple. XML's designers intended it to support much more sophisticated documents and used a very rigorous design process to achieve this goal. Understanding the design process will help you appreciate the types of application where XML can be helpful.

XML is based on a five-part conceptual model

The first step in the XML specification process was the definition of an underlying conceptual model. This model has five parts:

❑ Human and machine readability
❑ Defining content
❑ Defining structure
❑ Separation of content from relationships
❑ Separation of structure from presentation

As you will see, the XML syntax exemplified in the business card example is a result of these design goals.

Human and Machine Readability

Human and machine readability imposes syntactic constraints

One of the primary design goals behind XML was easy human reading and easy machine processing. This goal results in two different views of any particular document—the human view and the machine view. These views are subtly different, and providing a format that accommodates both views accounts for much of the XML syntax.

From the human perspective, the use of tag-based markup is a readable way to integrate metadata with content. From the machine perspective, parsing tag-based markup is simply one of many possible parsing tactics. Tag-based markup is a compromise that makes human reading easier without imposing too much of a burden on machine processing. On the other hand, a strict hierarchy of document elements is a compromise that makes machine processing easier without imposing too much of a burden on human reading. From the machine perspective, the use of a strict hierarchy makes it easy to create programming data structures from document content. From the human perspective, hierarchy is simply one of many possible organizational strategies. These two trade-offs have their roots in the human-machine duality. The human view is of a marked-up document; the machine view is of a tree of data.

Hierarchical tags represent a trade-off

In addition to being convenient from the machine perspective, hierarchy is generally a powerful organizational strategy. It can be used to represent both business concepts and programming data structures. Business process models, decision trees, and geographical models are all examples of business concepts that fit the hierarchical model. Trees, linked lists, and tables are all examples of programming data structures that can fit into a hierarchy.

Hierarchy is a powerful organizational strategy

Defining Content

A human reader may be able to decipher the implicit relationships among the words of a produce order such as, "100 10 pound bags carrots $1 per pound." However, a machine would have great difficulty with the same task. The human and machine readability goal necessitates a standard means of explicitly declaring the relationships among the words. Metadata enables a document author to specify these relationships in the document. Without metadata, the content of a document all looks the same; it's just a jumble of

Machines require explicit declaration of meaning

individual words. Because the content is homogeneous, it is meaningless.

XML uses elements
as the unit of content

In XML, authors define content as a set of elements. An element is a self-contained unit of content with a description of what the content means. For example, you could separate the preceding document into elements such as "Quantity = 100," "Size = 10," "Size Unit = pound," "Product = carrots," "Price Currency = $," "Price = 1," and "Pricing Unit = pound." Breaking the document into these elements would allow a human reader to interpret the order unambiguously and a machine to calculate the total price easily.

Defining Structure

XML uses hierarchy
to relate elements

With very simple documents, breaking content into elements may be sufficient by itself to make the document easily interpretable. However, even a modest document can become confusing without adding some structure to the content elements. Consider an expanded produce order such as, "100 10 pound bags carrots $1 per pound and 25 limes 50¢ per lime." With just a list of elements, how would you know which quantity and price applied to which product? How would you account for prices in different units? The solution is to structure the content so the relationships among content elements are easily apparent. As mentioned previously, XML uses a hierarchical structuring model. By organizing the expanded document into a hierarchy, you can now clearly apply the correct quantity and price to each product as shown in Example 2-2a.

Example 2-2a

Order
  Line Item
    Quantity = 100
    Product = carrots

Size = 10
   Size Unit = pound
 Price = 1
   Pricing Currency = dollars
   Pricing Unit = pound
Line Item
 Quantity = 25
 Product = limes
   Size = 1
   Size Unit = each
 Price = 50
   Pricing Currency = cents
   Pricing Unit = each

Unfortunately, a generic hierarchy is not specific enough to provide the shared context described in Chapter 1. Clearly, a produce order and a patient record each follow different rules. XML DTDs provide a means for specifying the rules that the hierarchy in a particular document must follow. These rules include the allowable element types at each level of the hierarchy. A pseudocode description of the rules governing the hierarchy for our example produce an order document that might look like Example 2-2b.

DTDs constrain element hierarchy

Example 2-2b
Top-level elements = exactly 1 "Order"
  Sub-element of "Order" is 1 or more "Line Item"
    Sub-element of "Line Item" is exactly 1 "Product"
      Sub-element of "Product" is exactly 1 "Size"
      Sub-element of "Product" is exactly 1 "Size Unit"
    Sub-element of "Line Item" is exactly 1 "Price"
      Sub-element of "Price" is exactly 1 "Price Currency"
      Sub-element of "Price" is exactly 1 "Price Unit"

Separation of Content from Relationships

Relationships between documents are important

Although hierarchical relationships among elements within a document are important, for many applications associative relationships among elements in different documents are also important. HTML links are an example of associative relationships between documents. As the success of the Web illustrates, there is often informational value in these associative relationships as well as document content. For example, a set of five Product, five Order, and five Customer documents is much more useful if you know which Orders relate to which Products and which Customers. Unfortunately, HTML embeds these important relationships within the document structure, making them difficult to maintain. The results are broken links and frustrating "HTTP 404—Object Not Found" errors.

XML separates content from relationships

In XML, document content and document relationships can be separate. Each is a first-class citizen of the XML paradigm. In XML, relationships can exist outside documents, making it possible to maintain the integrity of relationships independent of the documents and even introduce new relationships without affecting the referenced documents. This independence allows authors to create valuable information by relating documents in sophisticated ways, without ever changing the content of the related documents.

Separation of Structure from Presentation

HTML emphasizes document presentation

Another drawback of HTML is the primacy of presentation over structure. For example, to distinguish sections of a document, many authors have forsaken heading specifiers such as <H1> for direct control over font attributes such as <FONT SIZE=16>. This approach results in two problems. First, all content looks exactly the same. Second, readers are limited to the presentation imposed by the author.

In XML, document structure and document presentation are separate. Authors and readers have agreed that structured information
rather than page layout is the important item of exchange. Authors
may suggest a presentation, but readers are free to use whatever
presentations they choose. Different readers may use different presentations and the same reader may use different presentations
under different circumstances. Another advantage of this approach
is that it creates an opportunity for people to add value by creating
presentation styles independent of the document author.

*XML emphasizes
document structure*

Introducing Elements

The fundamental unit of XML content is the element—it is an
author-specified chunk of information. An element consists of an
element name and **element content**. XML is case sensitive, so you
must ensure that you pay attention to case when assigning element
names and creating element content. Start and end tags denote the
boundaries of the element and contain the element name. The element content may consist of character data or other elements. Consider the annotated version of our business card document.

*Elements are the
unit of content*

Example 2-3

```
<business_card>                                  root element
  <name>                                         element content
    <given_name>Kevin</given_name>               data content
    <middle_name>Stewart</middle_name>           data content
    <family_name>Dick</family_name>              data content
  </name>
  <title>Software Technology Analyst</title>     data content
  <author/>                                       empty content
  <contact_methods>
    <phone>650-555-5000</phone>                  data content
```

```
        <phone>650-555-5001</phone>              data content
      </contact_methods>
    </business_card>
```

There is always one root element

In Example 2-3, "business_card" is the top-level element. In XML, there can be only one element at the top level. This element is called the **root element** or **document element**. Think of this element as the trunk of the tree from which all other elements branch. Figure 2-2 shows the corresponding tree for Example 2-3 with each node representing an element and identified with the element name. The element content would be stored within the node.

There are four types of content

The annotations in Example 2-3 indicate the content model for each element. There are four types of allowable element content:

❑ **Data content.** These elements contain only data. Note that in the 1.0 version of the XML specification, there is no way to enforce datatype restrictions on data content such as integer, floating point, and date. Chapter 3 discusses a related standard, **XML Schema**, under development to address this potentially serious shortcoming.

❑ **Element content.** These elements contain only other elements.

Figure 2-2: Element tree

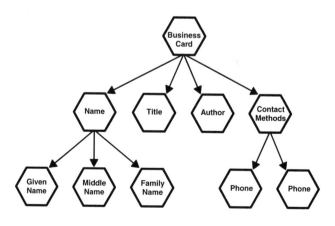

❏ **Empty.** These elements contain neither elements nor data.

❏ **Mixed content.** These elements contain both data and other elements. None of the elements in Example 2-3 have this type of element content because most XML experts feel using elements with mixed content is poor design practice when representing data.

Notice that, except for empty elements, all elements in Example 2-3 have a start tag and an end tag. The start tag is bounded by angle brackets, for example, <elementname>. The end tag is bounded by angle brackets and has a leading slash, as in </elementname>. All content, whether data or element, must occur between the start and end tags. An empty element has an empty tag, bounded by angle brackets with a trailing slash, for example, <elementname/>.

Nonempty elements must have start and end tags

XML limits the allowable syntax of a document. A document that obeys all the syntax rules is **well formed**. There are several technical criteria for well-formedness, but the primary ones are that

A document with the correct syntax is well formed

❏ There is one root element.

❏ All nonempty elements have start tags and end tags that match exactly.

❏ All empty elements have the correct empty tag syntax.

❏ Elements are strictly nested—there are no overlapping elements.

An XML processor can process a well-formed XML document unambiguously, building a tree data structure in which each node is an element that contains either data content, references to its subelements, both, or neither. You could use such documents to represent many different kinds of content. Example 2-4 shows a document that represents the schema for a simple contact database. Figure 2-3 shows the corresponding tree.

Well-formed documents are unambiguous

Example 2-4

```
<database>
  <table>
    <column>Name</column>
    <column>Phone Number</column>
  </table>
  <table>
    <column>Date</column>
    <column>Person</column>
  </table>
</database>
```

Element names don't provide enough information

Although the document in Example 2-4 captures the basic structure of the contact database, there is not enough information for a software program to process the document, establish a connection to the database in question, and perform queries. The element names "database," "table," and "column" are insufficiently descriptive. Clearly, you need a richer syntax for describing the metadata associated with an element.

Figure 2-3:
Database tree

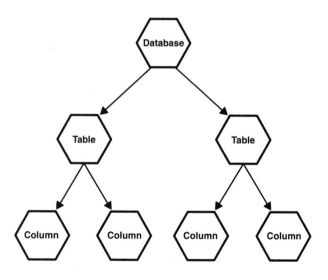

Introducing Attributes

Attributes provide the solution for adding richer metadata to elements. An attribute consists of an ***attribute name*** and an ***attribute
value***. The attribute value is bounded by quotation marks. This
attribute specification appears in the start tag of the element, and
you can specify as many attributes for an element as you feel necessary to describe it. As with all XML constructs, attribute names and
attribute values are case sensitive. As a stylistic convention, some
authors use uppercase text for attribute names so that they can easily distinguish between names of elements and names of attributes.
Example 2-5 shows how adding attributes to the contact database
might actually make it possible to use the database.

*Attributes provide
additional infor-
mation*

Example 2-5
```
<database DBTYPE="Oracle" ADDRESS="192.168.1.1">
  <table NAME="Person">
    <column DATATYPE="String">Name</column>
    <column DATATYPE="String">Phone Number</column>
  </table>
  <table NAME="Conversation">
    <column DATATYPE="Date">Date</column>
    <column DATATYPE="String">Person</column>
  </table>
</database>
```

Figure 2-4 shows the tree structure of this document. Note that it is
exactly the same as the tree structure in Figure 2-3.

*Attributes don't affect
the tree structure*

From Example 2-4 to Example 2-5, the element hierarchy did not
change. The element content did not even change. What did attributes add? They added metadata. They added information that will
allow consumers of the document, in this case database access programs, to use the content effectively. The "DBTYPE" attribute tells it

*Attributes provide
additional metadata*

**Figure 2-4: Database
tree with attributes**

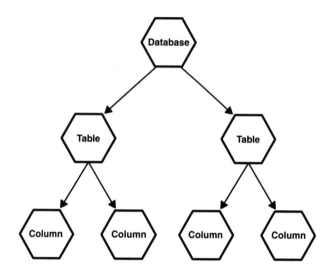

what database networking protocol to use. The "LOCATION" attribute tells it where to find the database. The "NAME" attribute tells it how to select the appropriate table. The "DATATYPE" attributes tell it how to form valid queries for each column. Obviously, a real version of this application might require even more attributes to work, but with XML, providing them would be easy.

Creating an "Order" in XML

*A complete example
illustrates the power
of XML*

The earlier examples in this chapter have used somewhat simplified XML documents. To get a proper feel for XML, it helps to see a realistic and complete document. Example 2-6 is a complete order for PC hardware in XML.

*The document prolog
appears first*

You can see immediately that it has some features not seen in previous examples. First, it starts with a *prolog*. The prolog is header information that appears before the root element. This particular prolog contains *a processing instruction* and a document type declaration. A processing instruction gives special information to software that may process the document. It starts with "<?" and ends with "?>." It has a target, in this case the XML processor itself, and one or more attribute-value pairs, in this case a version specification. A document may contain as many processing instructions as necessary, including different instructions for different applications that may process it. A document type declaration indicates the DTD to which the document complies and where to find it. It starts with "<!DOCTYPE" and ends with ">." It has the root element of the document, which must match an element defined in the DTD. It also has a place to look for the DTD, in this case the local filesystem, and a handle, in this case a filename. DTDs contain the rules that a document's elements must follow, which are discussed more fully in the next section.

The second new feature of Example 2-6 is that the body of the document starts with a comment, always a good idea with any software code. Comments can occur anywhere after the prolog. They start with "<!—" and end with "—>."

Comments can appear after the prolog

Example 2-6

```
<?xml version="1.0"?>
<!DOCTYPE order SYSTEM "order.dtd">
<!— Example Order Form from _XML: A Manager's Guide_ —>

<order SOURCE="web" CUSTOMERTYPE="consumer" CURRENCY=
"USD">
  <addresses>
    <address ADDTYPE="billship">
      <firstname>Kevin</firstname>
      <lastname>Dick</lastname>
      <street ORDER="1">123 Anywhere Lane</street>
      <street ORDER="2">Apt 1B</street>
      <city>Palo Alto</city>
```

```
          <state>CA</state>
          <postal>94303</postal>
          <country>USA</country>
        </address>
      </addresses>

      <lineitems>
        <lineitem ID="line1">
          <product CAT="Mboard">440BX Motherboard</product>
          <quantity>1</quantity>
          <unitprice>200</unitprice>
        </lineitem>

        <lineitem ID="line2">
          <product CAT="RAM">128 MB PC-100 DIMM</product>
          <quantity>2</quantity>
          <unitprice>175</unitprice>
        </lineitem>

        <lineitem ID="line3">
          <product CAT="CDROM">40x CD-ROM</product>
          <quantity>1</quantity>
          <unitprice>50</unitprice>
        </lineitem>
        <shipping>Federal Express</shipping>
      </lineitems>

      <payment>
        <card CARDTYPE="VISA">
          <cardholder>Kevin S Dick</cardholder>
          <number>41280000000000</number>
          <expiration>01/01</expiration>
        </card>
      </payment>
    </order>
```

After the comment comes the root element. In this case, the root element is "order." It has attributes that indicate where the order came from, the type of customer, and the currency for the quoted prices. The root element has three subelements, corresponding to the three major sections of an order—addresses, line items, and payment information.

The order element has three subelements

Most of the rest of the document is self-explanatory. However, there are a few interesting features. First, the "address" element has an "ADDTYPE" attribute, indicating that the contained address should be used as both the billing and shipping address. As you will see in the next section, the DTD will specify that this attribute must have one of the following values: "bill," "ship," and "billship." Using this approach of an attribute with an enumerated set of possible values is a common technique in designing XML documents. Another common technique is to use attributes to indicate the logical order of multiple elements in a list, such as the "ORDER" attribute of the "street" element.

The attributes help distinguish among elements

Another feature of note is the "ID" attribute of the "lineitem" element. As you will see in the next section, the DTD will specify that this attribute is of a special type—ID. ID attributes must be unique within the document, allowing software programs to use the attribute as an index when managing a group of the same elements. By convention, attributes of the ID type are often named "ID."

ID attributes serve as indexes

Introducing Document Types

From a business perspective, the single order document in Example 2-5 is obviously less useful in isolation than as a collection of many such documents. It would hardly make sense to write a piece of software that processed just one document or design a screen layout for displaying just one document. The true power of XML to

All order documents should use the same data format

improve business processes comes when multiple documents all use the same data format. Then a single piece of software can process them all and a single screen layout can display them all. Most important, if the format is publicly available, then anyone can generate a document that can be processed by the software or displayed in the screen layout.

DTDs enforce data formats

DTDs provide these common, public data formats. A DTD is a collection of rules that specifies the allowable structure of a class of documents. A DTD serves as a format referee at two important points in the software life cycle. During the design phase, a software developer can look at a DTD and know that as long as the application he builds will output documents that conform to that DTD, other applications can process those documents. During the execution phase, the XML processor can verify that a document conforms to the DTD, so the application that processes the document knows that it will receive only validly structured content. In essence, the DTD is a contract between the supplier of the document and the consumer. A particular XML document is said to be *valid* if it obeys all the rules of its parent DTD, as well as the criteria for well-formed documents.

DTDs indicate rules for elements and attributes

Earlier in the chapter, you saw that elements and attributes are the two primary constructs in an XML document. It shouldn't surprise you to learn that the syntax for DTDs deals primarily with specifying allowable element structure and rules that attributes must follow.

Defining Element Structure

A DTD specifies the shape of the document tree

In Example 2-1b, you saw a DTD for a simple business card that specified the shape of the document tree—the nodes and allowable branches from each node. In Example 2-7 this DTD is annotated to illustrate how to use DTD syntax to specify the different types of content.

Example 2-7

```
<!ELEMENT business_card (name, title, author,
contact_methods)>                        root element

<!ELEMENT name (given_name, middle_name?,
family_name)>                            element content
<!ELEMENT given_name (#PCDATA)>          data content
<!ELEMENT middle_name (#PCDATA)>         data content
<!ELEMENT family_name (#PCDATA)>         data content

<!ELEMENT title (#PCDATA)>               data content

<!ELEMENT author EMPTY>                  empty content

<!ELEMENT contact_methods (phone*)>      element content
<!ELEMENT phone (#PCDATA)>               data content
```

Each *element declaration* begins with "<!ELEMENT" and ends with ">." It contains the element name and a *content model* surrounded by parentheses. As we saw earlier, there are four types of allowable content. The corresponding syntax for each content models is as follows:

Each content model has corresponding DTD syntax

- ❑ **Data content.** These elements contain only data. To indicate this structure, the element declaration specifies a content model of *PCDATA.*

- ❑ **Element content.** These elements contain only other elements. To indicate this structure, the element declaration specifies a content model that lists the element names, separated by commas. Note that this list is order sensitive.

- ❑ **Empty.** These elements contain neither elements nor data. To indicate this structure, the element declaration uses the keyword EMPTY as the content model.

❏ **Mixed content.** These elements contain both data and other elements. To indicate this structure, the element declaration specifies a content model that includes #PCDATA to indicate that data content is allowed and element names to indicate that elements of these types are allowed.

The element model always starts with the root element

In defining the element model, a document designer starts with the root element. After the root element, the designer moves on to the subelements of the root elements. Then come the subelements of those elements, continuing until there are only leaf elements— ones that have only data content or are empty.

Designers can specify the number of times an element may appear

In addition to these basic content models, DTD designers may use special characters to encode rules about the number of subelements that an element may contain. These cardinality rules use the following syntax. Note that the default cardinality is exactly 1:

❏ **0 or 1.** The ? character indicates an optional subelement. So <!ELEMENT person (firstname, middlename?, lastname)> indicates that person must have one "firstname," then may or may not have one "middlename," then must have one "lastname."

❏ **0 or more.** The * character indicates a subelement that may appear one or more times. So <!ELEMENT contact_methods (phone_number*)> indicates that "contact methods" may have any number of "phone_numbers."

❏ **1 or more.** The + character indicates a subelement that must appear at least once. So <!ELEMENT contact_methods (phone_number+)> would indicate that there must be at least one phone number.

❏ **Enumerated alternatives.** A list of subelements separated by vertical bars indicates that the element must contain one of the subelements in the list. So, <!ELEMENT payment (cash |

check | charge)> would indicate that "payment" must contain
either "cash," "check," or "charge."

Rules may nest

Document designers can combine different rules in the same element declaration, using parentheses to group subelements together.
For example, <!ELEMENT workid (passport | (driverslicense,
socialsecuritycard))> indicates that acceptable "workid" consists of
either a "passport" or both a "driverslicense" and a "socialsecurity
card." The declaration <!ELEMENT e-maillist (name?, (mailserver,
to+, cc*)+, (version | updated))> indicates that an "emaillist" has
(1) an optional "name"; (2) one or more blocks that include one
"mailserver"; one or more "to," and zero or more "cc"; and
(3) either a "version" or an "updated." As you can see, the syntax
for defining element structure is rich enough to make plain English
descriptions difficult. These basic building blocks give you the
power to specify sophisticated content models.

Defining Attribute Rules

As you've already learned, elements are only one of the primary
constructs available to XML document authors. Attributes enhance
the meaning of element content by providing additional metadata.
Not surprisingly, XML DTDs include syntax for defining the rules
that attributes must follow. Example 2-8 is a DTD for the database
schema definition document from Example 2-5. As you can see, the
element declarations specify a database root element with one or
more table elements. Each table element must have one or more
column elements, each of which has character data.

*A DTD also specifies
allowable attributes*

Example 2-8

```
<!ELEMENT database (table+)>
<!ELEMENT table (column+)>
<!ELEMENT column (#PCDATA)>
```

```
<!ATTLIST database
DBTYPE        CDATA              #REQUIRED
ADDRESS       CDATA              #IMPLIED >
<!ATTLIST table
NAME          CDATA              #REQUIRED>
<!ATTLIST column
DATATYPE      (String | Int | Float | Date | BLOB) "String">
```

Attribute declara-
tions have four parts

Remember that in Example 2-5 attributes were added to an existing set of elements. Therefore, in addition to element declarations, Example 2-8 includes attribute declarations that define the rules that these attributes must follow. These declarations begin with <!ATTLIST and end with ">." Internally, they have four parts:

❏ **Element type.** After the ATTLIST keyword, the declaration specifies the element to which the list applies. In Example 2-8, the "database," "table" and "column" elements have attribute list declarations.

❏ **Attribute name.** The rule for each attribute in the list appears on a new line. The first part of the rule is the attribute name. For example, the "database" element has "DBTYPE" and "ADDRESS" attributes.

❏ **Attribute type.** After the attribute name, the type specification of the attribute appears. For character values such as "DBTYPE" and "ADDRESS," the type specification is *CDATA* For enumerated values such as "DATATYPE," the type specification is a list of the possible values, separated by a vertical bar and enclosed in parentheses. Not appearing in Example 2-8 are the ID and IDREF type specifications. ID indicates a character string that is unique for all elements within the document. IDREF indicates a character string that corresponds to the value of an ID attribute within the document. Using ID and IDREF attributes, document authors can create links between elements in the same document.

❏ **Default value.** After the attribute type, the document designer must specify the default value for the attribute. There are a number of options. #REQUIRED indicates that every document must explicitly assign a value to the attribute. "DBTYPE" is an example of a #REQUIRED attribute. #IMPLIED indicates that a document does not have to assign a value to the attribute; the XML processor will tell the application that no value was assigned. "ADDRESS" is an example of an #IMPLIED attribute. A value in quotation marks indicates an attribute with a default value; if the document does not explicitly assign a value to the attribute, the XML processor will automatically assign the default value. "DATATYPE" has the default value "String." Not appearing in Example 2-8 are attributes with #FIXED default actions. After the #FIXED keyword, there is an attribute value in quotation marks. If a document explicitly assigns a value to such an attribute, it must be the same as the value specified after #FIXED.

DTDs give document designers a high degree of control over both the structure of document elements and the rules element attributes must follow. This control opens the doors for document designers to create DTDs that apply to vastly different fields, from online catalogs, to supply chain management systems, to database integration tools.

DTDs are a powerful tool

Example DTD

Examples 2-7 and 2-8 demonstrate the syntax for specifying element structure and attribute rules for simple DTDs. Even DTDs for modest applications such as the order form in Example 2-6 can quickly become complex. To illustrate the potential complexity of a DTD for a complete XML application, Example 2-9 consists of a DTD for this order form.

A complete DTD illustrates it's expressive power

Example 2-9

```
<!— Example Order Form DTD from _XML: A Manager's Guide_ —>
<!— Document Structure —>
<!ELEMENT order (addresses, lineitems, payment)>

<!— Collection of Addresses —>
<!ELEMENT addresses (address+)>

<!— Address Structure —>
<!ELEMENT address (firstname, middlename?, lastname, street+,
city, state, postal, country)>
<!ELEMENT firstname (#PCDATA)>
<!ELEMENT middlename (#PCDATA)>
<!ELEMENT lastname (#PCDATA)>
<!ELEMENT street (#PCDATA)>
<!ELEMENT city (#PCDATA)>>
<!ELEMENT state (#PCDATA)>
<!ELEMENT postal (#PCDATA)>
<!ELEMENT country (#PCDATA)>

<!— Collection of Lineitems —>
<!ELEMENT lineitems (lineitem+)>

<!— Lineitem Structure —>
<!ELEMENT lineitem (product, quantity, unitprice)>
<!ELEMENT product(#PCDATA)>
<!ELEMENT quantity(#PCDATA)>
<!ELEMENT unitprice(#PCDATA)>

<!— Payment Structure —>
<!ELEMENT payment (card | PO)>
```

```
<!— Card Structure —>
<!ELEMENT card (cardholder, number, expiration)>
<!ELEMENT cardholder (#PCDATA)>
<!ELEMENT number (#PCDATA)>
<!ELEMENT expiration (#PCDATA)>


<!— PO Structure —>


<!ELEMENT PO (number, authorization*)>
<!ELEMENT number (#PCDATA)>
<!ELEMENT authorization (#PCDATA)>


<!— Attribute Rules —>
<!ATTLIST order
SOURCE          (web | phone | retail )      #REQUIRED
CUSTOMERTYPE    (consumer | business)        "consumer"
CURRENCY        CDATA                        "USD">
<!ATTLIST address
ADDTYPE         (bill | ship | billship)     "billship">
<!ATTLIST street
ORDER           CDATA                        #IMPLIED>
<!ATTLIST lineitem
ID              ID                           #REQUIRED>
<!ATTLIST product
CAT             (CDROM | MBoard | RAM)       #REQUIRED>
<!ATTLIST card
CARDTYPE        (VISA | MasterCard | Amex)   #REQUIRED>
```

The root element for this DTD is "order" and it has three required subelements: "addresses," "lineitems," and "payment." The "addresses" and "lineitems" elements are simply collections of one or more "address" and "lineitem" elements, respectively. Therefore, "addresses" and "lineitems" are not strictly necessary. The "order"

DTD designers should plan for extensibility

43

element could contain the collections of "address" and "lineitem" elements directly. In this case, the first element declaration would be <!ELEMENT order (address+, lineitem+, payment)>. However, at some point in the future, the application may need additional information that applies to a group of "address" or "lineitem" elements. Suppose that the company develops a pricing strategy that allows sales representatives to apply different discount policies to different blocks of lineitems. In this case, you would need to allow multiple "lineitems" elements and add a "discountpolicy" subelement to " lineitems." The syntax for these changes would be <!ELEMENT order (addresses, lineitems+, payment)> and <!ELEMENT lineitems (discountpolicy?, lineitems+)>, respectively. Notice that, because the "discountpolicy" element is optional, all documents that conform to the original DTD will also conform to the new DTD. Planning for this future enhancement is an important part of DTD design.

This DTD leaves room for multiple authorizations

Beyond this subtle design point, the rest of the element structure is relatively straightforward. The other interesting features of the element structure are in the "payment" element. This element presents a binary decision between the credit card and purchase order payment methods with the "card" and "PO" subelements. The "PO" subelement allows for an optional list of "authorization" elements. This list enables the application to keep track of anyone at the customer who authorized the PO. If there is a dispute about payment, maintaining this information could be very important.

You should specify default values where appropriate

The attribute specification reveals the flexibility of the rules document designers may apply. "CURRENCY" and "ORDER" may both have character data values, but "CURRENCY" has a default value whereas "ORDER" is completely optional. "SOURCE," "ADDTYPE," "CAT," and "CARDTYPE" are all enumerated types, but the document must explicitly assign an option to "SOURCE," "CAT," and

"CARDTYPE" while "ADDTYPE" has a default value. The required "ID" attribute of ID type for the "lineitem" element enables an application using an order document to uniquely identify any particular "lineitem" element with its "ID" attribute.

Although the DTD in Example 2-9 is somewhat long and modestly complex, in comparison with DTDs used in actual applications, it is still relatively simple. You could imagine the necessary complexity of DTDs for documents in financial wire transfer, telecommunications service provisioning, and medical record applications. Designing DTDs that cover all the possible document cases as well as allowing for future enhancements is one of the crucial processes in deploying effective XML applications.

DTDs for real applications can be very complex

Introducing Entities

Elements and attributes are primarily logical mechanisms. They enable authors to specify the logical meaning of document content. On the other hand, *entities* are primarily structural mechanisms. They enable authors to manipulate the physical structure of documents. As physical concepts, entities are interesting mostly to programmers. However, they do provide useful features for organizing XML documents and you should have a high-level understanding of how they work.

Entities are structural mechanisms

An entity associates an *entity name* with a fragment of content. Authors define entities with an !ENTITY declaration at the beginning of a document or DTD. There are four types of entities in XML, three that apply to documents and one that applies to DTDs:

An entity is a fragment of content

❑ **Internal parsed entities.** These entities allow authors to define an alias for a fragment of text within a document. So the declaration <!ENTITY author "Kevin Dick"> would allow me to type "&author" within a document and have it replaced by "Kevin Dick" when the document was processed. Using internal entities can reduce the size of documents by replacing large pieces of recurring text with a shorter name. It also makes documents more extensible. If I decided that I wanted my name to appear as "Kevin S. Dick," I would have to change only the !ENTITY declaration.

❑ **External parsed entities.** These entities allow authors to include an entire file as part of a document. Using external entities, we could decompose the order document from Example 2-6 into three components:

```
<!ENTITY address_section SYSTEM "./address.xml">
<!ENTITY lineitems_section SYSTEM "./lineitems.xml">
<!ENTITY payment_section SYSTEM "./payment.xml">
&address_section;
&lineitems_section;
&payment_section;
```

Such a decomposition would be useful for managing long documents. It would also be useful if different authors were responsible for creating different parts of the document. They could work on these files independently without worrying about overlapping changes.

❑ **Unparsed entities.** These entities allow authors to insert arbitrary data in a document. This data may not be XML. It may not even be text. The XML processor will not attempt to parse such an entity.

❑ **Parameter entities.** These entities work only within DTDs. They enable the DTD designer to create reusable and extensible design elements for document structure. Remember the DTD for our order document in Example 2-9. One of the attributes of the "card" element was "CARDTYPE." This attribute provided a list of acceptable credit cards:

CARDTYPE (VISA | MasterCard | Amex) #REQUIRED

What if the company using this DTD decided to take Discover cards as well? This company might have many other document types with the same information. A parameter entity would allow DTD designers a means to update the acceptable cards at the beginning of each document:

```
<!ENTITY % card_list "VISA | MasterCard | Amex | Discover">
CARDTYPE (%card_list;) #REQUIRED>
```

Although XML documents and DTDs deliver significant benefits in exchanging information, it's only natural to want to enhance these capabilities even further. Much as with peeling an onion, addressing the most visible information exchange problem on the Internet reveals further possibilities for improvement. Chapter 3 introduces some of the related standards that are emerging to address these possibilities.

XML itself is just the beginning

Technical Summary

❏ An element consists of open and close tags containing the element name surrounding the element content—<element_name>element content</element_name>.

❏ Attributes appear in the open tag and consist of an attribute name and an attribute value—<element_name ATTRIBUTE_NAME = "attribute_value">.

❏ For elements with element content, a DTD specifies the allowable child elements—<!ELEMENT element_name (child_1* child_2? child_3+)>.

❏ *, ?, and + indicate the number of times an element may occur—0 or more, 0 or 1, and 1 or more, respectively. The default is exactly 1.

❑ For elements with data content, a DTD specifies the type of data it may contain—<!ELEMENT element_name (#PCDATA)>.

❑ For elements with no content, a DTD specifies an empty content model—<!ELEMENT element_name EMPTY>.

❑ For elements with attributes, a DTD specifies the list of allowable attributes—

```
<!ATTLIST element_name
ATTRIBUTE_NAME_1 CDATA "default">
ATTRIBUTE_NAME_2 CDATA #REQUIRED
ATTRIBUTE_NAME_3 (option_1 | option_2 | option_3 )
"option_1">
```

❑ Default attribute values appear within quotation marks.

❑ DTDs can require documents to assign an attribute value explicitly with the "#REQUIRED" keyword.

❑ DTDs can specify an enumerated list of allowable attribute values bounded by parentheses with options separated by vertical bars.

3

Related Standards

Executive Summary

XML documents and DTDs provide the foundation for an Internet document paradigm. However, by themselves, documents and DTDs do not provide all the necessary features of such a paradigm. Moreover, as people have begun to use documents and DTDs, they have discovered drawbacks they would like to avoid. These two factors have led to several related standards efforts. Table 3-1 lists some of the most important ones.

Related standards add capabilities to XML

As you can see, most of the standards related to XML were still being defined at the time of this writing. Undoubtedly, as new requirements for Internet documents emerge, additional standards will also emerge. Clearly, making use of a standard that is not finalized increases the level of project risk. Balancing this risk with the

The XML standards family is constantly evolving

Table 3-1: Standards efforts

Standard	Abbreviation	Specification Status	Purpose
XML Namespaces	Namespaces	Recommendation	Prevent overlap of names used by different software
XML Linking Language	XLink	Working Draft	Flexible document linking
Extensible Stylesheet Language	XSL	Working Draft	Flexible document presentation
XSL Transformations	XSLT	Working Draft	Easy transformation of XML content from one data format to another
XML Schema	N/A	Working Draft	More extensive document definition rules than DTDs

benefits provided by new capabilities requires some understanding of what the standard proposes to do and the potential for evolution of the specification. The rest of this chapter reviews the important details of the standards listed in Table 3-1.

Overview of Namespaces

Applications associate an element's content with its element name

As you saw in the previous chapter, the primary unit of content in XML is the element. Authors distinguish among element types by using a unique element name. When applications process a document, they associate the element content with the corresponding element name.

Two applications may process the same document

In many cases, a single document may contain information relevant to multiple applications. For example, most vendors may not charge customers for goods until they ship the goods. This policy requires processing of the same information by an Accounting application for billing purposes and a Fulfillment application for shipping purposes.

The same term may have different meanings to different applications

A primary goal of XML is to enable the effective integration of information across such applications. But what if the Accounting and Fulfillment applications use the term "status" to signify different meanings? Both applications want their respective status data associated with the "status" element name. Such a **naming collision** has the potential to make life very uncomfortable for developers responsible for specifying the formats of affected documents.

Namespaces eliminate naming collisions

XML Namespaces, a W3C Recommendation, enables developers to avoid naming collisions by assigning element and attribute names to *namespaces*. So Accounting and Fulfillment departments could each have separate namespaces. Developers can thereby qualify the use of the "status" element name with the appropriate namespace.

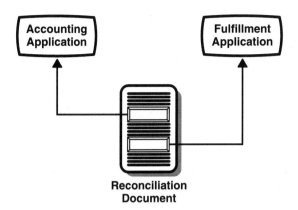

Figure 3-1: Resolving a conflict with name-spaces

Reconciliation Document

How It Works

Figure 3-1 helps illustrate how namespaces can resolve the conflict between the Accounting and Fulfillment applications. A Reconciliation Document consolidates all billing and shipping information about a given order. When the billing status is "invoiced" and the shipping status is "shipped," the document goes to both the Accounting and Fulfillment applications.

When the Accounting application processes the document, it wants to use "status" as a keyword to signify billing status. When the Fulfillment application processes the document, it wants to use "status" as a keyword to signify shipping status. Moreover, the same problem extends to other keywords. Example 3-1 shows how to solve this problem using XML Namespaces.

Example 3-1

```
<acct:customer xmlns:acct="http://www.foocompany.com/
names/acct-REV10">
  <acct:name>Bar Corporation</acct:name>
  <acct:addressee>Accounts Payable—Bar Corporation</acct:
  addressee>
  <acct:order acct:reference="5566-1010">
```

```
        <acct:status>invoice</acct:status>
      </acct:order>
    </acct:customer>
    <ful:customer xmlns:ful="http://www.foocompany.com/names/
    ful-REV10">
      <ful:name>Bar Corporation</ful:name>
      <ful:addressee>Loading Dock</ful:addressee>
      <ful:order ful:reference="A9875656">
        <ful:status>shipped</ful:status>
      </ful:order>
    </ful:customer>
```

A namespace can apply to elements and attributes

As you can see, attaching the namespace to an element or attribute name with a colon associates that namespace with that element or attribute. The first time you use a namespace, you associate the **namespace prefix** with the **namespace name** using the reserved XML attribute "xmlns." The namespace name is a **Uniform Resource Identifier** (URI), essentially indicating that the owner of an Internet resource is the owner of the namespace. In this case, "acct" signifies the namespace owned by the Accounting department of Foo Company and "ful" signifies the namespace owned by the Fulfillment department of Foo Company.

You can also set a default namespace

When a single namespace applies to an element and all of its child elements, attaching the prefix to all element and attribute names can be cumbersome. To avoid this chore, you can also set a default namespace, which applies to all contained names, as shown in Example 3-2.

Example 3-2

```
<customer xmlns="http://www.foocompanycom/names/
acct-REV10">
  <name>Bar Corporation</name>
```

```
<addressee>Accounts Payable—Bar Corporation</addressee>
<order reference="5566-1010">
  <status>invoice</status>
</order>
</customer>
<customer xmlns="http://www.foocompany.com/names/
ful-REV10">
  <name>Bar Corporation</name>
  <addressee>Loading Dock</addressee>
  <order reference="A9875656">
    <status>shipped</status>
  </order>
</customer>
```

In Example 3-2, we first set a default Accounting namespace by specifying the value of the "xmlns" attribute without attaching a namespace prefix to the element name. All names within the "customer" element automatically use the Accounting namespace. Then we set a default namespace Fulfillment and define all the elements that use that namespace. You can also set a default namspace and then use the syntax in Example 3-1 to specify a different namespace for particular elements or attributes. The combination of the two mechanisms for specifying namespaces delivers a convenient and flexible way to avoid naming collisions.

You can reset the default namespace within a document

Overview of XLink

It makes sense to define a companion linking standard for XML. Many people want to use XML on the Web, where linking is an absolute requirement. Also, once people can easily exchange and understand structured documents, specifying relationships among them becomes very valuable. These forces have led to the **XML Linking Language (XLink)** initiative. At the time of this writing,

Web documents and linking often go together

XLink was in the Working Draft stage of the W3C process, but it will no doubt become a Recommendation in the near future.

XLink is backward compatible with HTML links

The Web is a primary target for XML application. Most Web authors are familiar with HTML and its **link** syntax. Therefore, a goal of the XLink specification is to make it very straightforward to use this syntax to create a one-way link from a point in an XML source document to a target document. This compatibility lowers the learning barrier for existing Web developers.

XLink enables multiple target documents from the same link

However, XLink goes beyond simple HTML links. XML makes it easy to exchange structured information. But people often want to relate different pieces of information in different ways. Therefore, XLink enables people to specify links with multiple target documents.

An application could consist of just creating links

Suppose that an attorney has researched a particular esoteric and complex point of the law. Parts of many different court opinions apply in differing degrees to this attorney's particular case. With XLink, the attorney could create an extended link that led to all the different opinions, categorized the opinions by relevance, and pointed to specific passages in the opinions. The attorney could then e-mail this extended link to other attorneys on the case. Or consider an order processing application whose only function is creating two sets of links. To the Shipping department, it e-mails a set of links from the shipping address element within a customer document to product number elements within product documents. To the Accounting department, it e-mails a set of links from the account number element within the customer document to the price elements within product documents.

How It Works

Simple links are like HTML links

Links with multiple targets are an exciting development, but let's start with the simple case. If you wanted to link just one Order Doc-

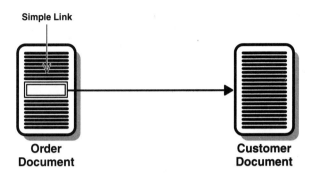

Figure 3-2: A simple link targeting the Customer Document

ument to one Customer Document, you would use a *simple link*. A simple link is very similar to a standard HTML link. Figure 3-2 shows how the link is defined as part of the Order Document and targets the Customer Document.

The syntax for a link is itself XML. Therefore, extracting the linking information from a document does not require any additional capabilities. However, knowing what to do with this information requires an XLink processor that understands what to do with the linking information. Document viewers such as Web browsers therefore need to include such a component to support links.

XLinks are defined with XML syntax

To separate the link information from the rest of the document, you would use the XLink namespace maintained by the W3C. Attaching "xlink:" to the linking attributes of an element ensures that the XLink processor receives the information as shown in Example 3-3.

XLink uses Namespaces

Example 3-3

```
<BarCorpLink
  xlink:form="simple"
  xlink:inline="true"
  xlink:href="http://www.foocompany.com/customers/
  barcorp.xml"
```

```
        xlink:role="link record"
        xlink:title="Bar Corporation"
        xlink:show="new"
        xlink:actuate="user"
        xlink:content-role="link BarCorp record"
        xlink:content-title="Link to Bar Corporation Customer Record">
        Bar Corporation
</BarCorpLink>
```

A simple link is a set of attributes

This XLink comprises a set of attributes on an element. The "inline" attribute indicates whether the element contents, in this case "Bar Corporation," are themselves part of the link. The "form" attribute specifies that this link is a simple link. The "href" attribute specifies the URI of the target document.

Attributes indicate desired behavior and provide semantic information

In addition to these basic attributes, there are special attributes to indicate the desired behavior for the link. The "show" attribute instructs the processor to open a new window for the target document. The "actuate" attribute instructs the processor to activate the link when the user clicks on it. The rest of the attributes provide the XLink processor with semantic information about the link. The interpretation of behavior and semantic attributes may be specific to a particular XLink processor.

Extended links enable separation of relationships from content

As shown in Figure 3-3, ***extended links*** allow multiple target documents. In this example, a Tracking Document associates the corresponding Invoice Document and Shipping Document. This Tracking Document contains only this link. So even though the Tracking Document is a valid XML document, it is logically independent of the content it connects. This separation of relationships from content is a powerful tool for categorizing content on the Web. For a given set of logical documents, there may be dozens of different categorizations, all implemented with links and all independent of each other.

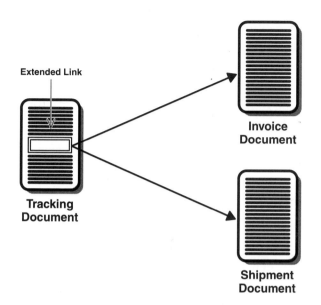

Figure 3-3: An extended link targeting multiple documents

Example 3-4

```
<BarCorpOrderTrackingLink
  xlink:form="extended"
  xlink:inline="false"
  xlink:role="track order"
  xlink:content-role"track BarCorp">
    <Invoice
      xlink:form="locator"
      xlink:href="BarCorpInvoice.xml"
      xlink:title="Bar Corporation Invoice"
      xlink:actuate="user"/>
    <Shipment
      xlink:form="locator"
      xlink:href="BarCorpShipment.xml"
      xlink:title="Bar Corporation Shipment"
      xlink:actuate="user"/>
</BarCorpOrderTrackingLink>
```

Extended links have components for each target document

Example 3-4 shows the syntax for an extended link. An extended link has "form" and "inline" attributes, as well as ones that indicate semantic information about the entire link. Then the link has subelements for each target document. These subelements have attributes indicating the location of each target, the desired behavior when connecting to the target, and semantic information specific to that part of the link.

XPointer enables linking to a specific element

Although not shown in any of these examples, *XML Pointer Language* (XPointer) enables you to target a specific element within a document. Unlike HTML, with which you have to declare a "NAME" attribute explicitly, XPointer enables you to specify them based on the structure of the document. For example, suppose you wanted to link to an order document valid in terms of the DTD in Example 2-9. Moreover, you wanted to link specifically to the shipping address. You could do so with the XPointer, "root().child(1,addresses).child (1,address,ADDTYPE,ship)." This code selects the first "addresses" child element of the root element. It then selects the first "address" child element whose "ADDTYPE" attribute is "ship." If for some reason, the document author changed the order of the addresses so that the billing address came first, this XPointer would still resolve to the correct location.

Overview of XSL

Document presentation is also important on the Web

As with linking, document presentation is an important part of the Web environment. So while specifying content independent of presentation is one XML's most important features, authors still require a means of formatting document display for users. **Extensible Stylesheet Language (XSL)** fulfills this need.

XSL applies formatting independent of content

The goal of XSL is to specify a language that allows people to apply formatting to XML documents without contaminating logical document content. There are three primary requirements for a solution:

❑ **Apply formatting rules to elements.** Authors can specify complete formatting rules for each type of element in a document. These rules include font format, indentation, line spacing, leading and trailing space, table formatting, and so on. Applying formatting rules to elements makes it very efficient to create stylesheets in conjunction with DTDs. Because all DTDs have the same structure, it makes sense that they should have the same formatting rules.

❑ **Usable with different display technologies.** The same stylesheet can render the same document using a variety of page layout languages such as **HTML**, **PDF**, **Postscript**, and **RTF**. Therefore, applying a **stylesheet** to a document creates an intermediate layout description called a *formatting object tree*. Then a renderer converts the formatting object tree into a specific page description language.

❑ **Document consumer may control application of stylesheets.** In HTML, the document author controls how the document consumer sees the document. However, in the XSL model, consumers may choose to apply any stylesheet they wish. A particular XSL filter could use large fonts if you are nearsighted or avoid particular colors if you are color blind. It could also suppress content not relevant to your particular needs. Once standard DTDs become adopted for things like personal information and product catalogs, there will probably be a host of stylesheets available designed by graphic artists.

How It Works

The basic concept of XSL stylesheets is relatively straightforward, but the implementation can be rather complicated. The fundamental idea is that different people want to view documents differently. They may have physical differences such as small versus large screen or poor versus good eyesight.

The concept is simple but the details are complex

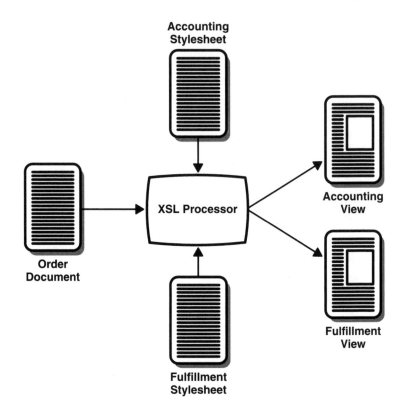

Figure 3-4: The XSL processor generating different views

XSL can provide customized views of information

People may also have logical differences. In Figure 3-4, employees in the Accounting department and Fulfillment department want to view the same Order Document differently. Accounting employees want emphasis on the billing address of the customer and Fulfillment employees want emphasis on the shipping address. They can each define their own stylesheet and the XSL processor can generate different page layouts for the same document.

Stylesheets can work independently of page layout language

Beyond the differences in how the Accounting and Fulfillment employees want the information formatted, there is another level of complexity. What if different people in the two departments use different document viewing technologies? Some may use HTML and others may use PDF. Therefore, the stylesheet must specify for-

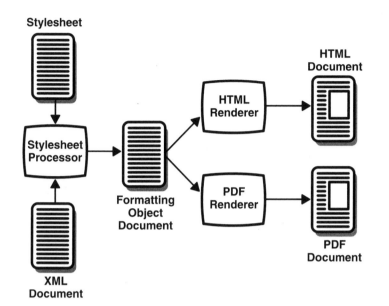

Stylesheet

Stylesheet Processor

XML Document

Formatting Object Document

HTML Renderer

PDF Renderer

HTML Document

PDF Document

Figure 3-5: The stylesheet processor generating different formats

matting independent of viewing technology. Figure 3-5 shows how the stylesheet processor generates an intermediate representation of the document as formatting objects. Then renderers translate these formatting objects into the syntax of different page layout languages.

Example 3-5 shows the syntax you would use to emphasize billing address over shipping address for the Accounting department, using the Order Document in Example 2-6. With XSL, you define formatting templates that apply to an element and its subelements. This simple stylesheet has two templates. Note that instructions for selecting the particular elements use the "xsl" namespace, whereas instruction for formatting output use the "fo" namespace.

You define formatting rules with XSL

The first template selects all "address" elements. For each child element, it starts a new paragraph, in large, bold, Arial type with double line spacing. The "apply-templates" syntax applies this formatting to all children of the "address" element, including the "firstname," "lastname," "street," "city," "state," "postal" and "country" elements.

The first template applies to all addresses

61

The second rule overrides formatting for shipping addresses

The second rule selects only those "address" elements whose "ADDTYPE" attributes are "ship." For each child element, it starts a new paragraph in small, normal, Times type with single line spacing. The more specific template selecting for shipping addresses overrides the general template for addresses. Therefore, addresses for billing or billing and shipping appear in large, bold type. Addresses for shipping only appear in small, plain type.

Example 3-5

```
<xsl:template match="address">
  <fo:block
     fo:font-size="large"
     fo:font-weight="bold"
     fo:font-family="Arial"
     fo:line-height="2"
     <xsl:apply-templates/>
   </fo:block>
</xsl:template>

<xsl:template match="address[@ADDTYPE="ship"]">
<fo:block
     fo:font-size="small"
     fo:font-weight="normal"
     fo:font-family="Times"
     fo:line-height="1"
     <xsl:apply-templates/>
   </fo:block>
</xsl:template>
```

XSL stylesheets are written using XML syntax

As you can see, XSL stylesheets are themselves XML documents, reusing all of the processing software for XML. The elements they output, such as the "paragraph" element, are formatting objects.

These formatting objects are in essence a general page description language that renderers translate into specific page description languages. One of the time-consuming parts of defining the XSL standard has been defining all of the allowable formatting objects.

Many XML authors are currently avoiding the use of formatting objects altogether. They use the XSL template syntax, but instead of using formatting objects, they directly insert HTML tags. In essence, they use XSL simply as a transformation language to transform the elements of the source document into elements of HTML. This concept of transformation applies in a general sense to converting documents from one format to another.

Authors can transform XML directly into HTML

Overview of XSLT

The general XSL approach of selecting elements on the basis of specific criteria can also help address a different problem. The proliferation of different DTDs for the same logical type of document can pose severe headaches for managers developing applications that must exchange such documents. Such a scenario is highly likely in applications such as supply chain management where two companies want to exchange conceptually the same information but already have DTDs that they use internally. Also, industry groups in finance, telecommunications, and transportation are defining DTDs for transactions in those industries. In some cases, multiple industry groups are working on the same problem, creating the potential for dueling standards.

Competing DTDs is a potential problem

In recognition of this problem, many XML professionals would like a straightforward means of transforming documents from one data format to another. XSL already seems to have many of the building blocks. It has mechanisms for searching through XML documents to locate specific elements. It has mechanisms for outputting new

XSL has many of the features necessary to solve this problem

documents on the basis of this processing. What if, instead of generating a formatting object document, we generated a plain old XML document?

XSLT is the subset of XSL for transforming XML documents

The result of this observation is **XSL Transformations (XSLT)**, a subset of XSL suitable for transforming an XML document in one format to an XML document in another format. Although XSLT is also in the Working Draft stage, it may achieve standardization faster than XSL because it doesn't have to define an exhaustive set of formatting objects.

How It Works

Two companies have different DTDs for orders

Consider the basic problem of automatically placing an order over the Internet. Foo Company has defined a Foo Company Order DTD that it uses internally. Bar has defined a Bar Corp Order DTD that it uses internally. Now Foo Company wants to place orders automatically with Bar Corp.

An XSLT document translates orders from one format to another

When Foo Company creates a Foo Company Order Document, it is valid with respect to the Foo Company Order DTD. However, for Bar Company to accept the order, the order document must be valid with respect to the Bar Corp Order DTD. To achieve this end, Foo Company creates a Foo Bar Transformation document that specifies how to translate a Foo Company Order Document into a Bar Corp Order Document as shown in Figure 3-6.

One document uses an attribute, another uses a child element

To see how XSLT works, let's consider a simple example. Examples 3-6a and 3-6b show parts of order documents in two different formats. Example 3-6a models currency information as an attribute on the "order" element. Example 3-6b models currency information as a child element of the "order" element. The choice of modeling information as an attribute or child element is a common one, and it is likely that two different DTDs for the same concept

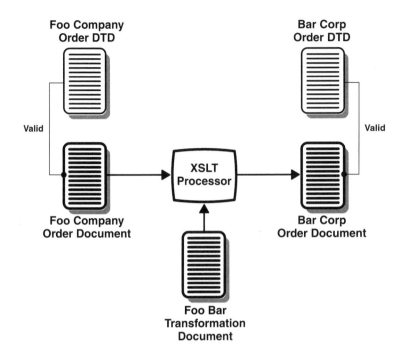

Figure 3-6: Translating documents

would choose different modeling techniques for at least one piece of information.

Example 3-6a

```
<order currency="USD">
. . .
</order>
```

Example 3-6b

```
<order>
  <currency>USD</currency>
. . .
</order>
```

Example 3-7 is the XSLT code for performing the transformation. Note the use of the XSL namespace to denote the elements using

The XSLT document inserts the attribute value as element content

XSL-specific constructs. The transformation document selects the "order" element in the source document. It then begins a new "order" element with a new "currency" child element in the translated document. It inserts the value of the "currency" attribute of the selected order element in the source document as the element content of the "currency" element in the translated document.

Example 3-7

```
<xsl:template match="/">
  <xsl:for-each select="order">
    <order>
      <currency>
        <xsl:value-of select="@currency"/>
      </currency>
    </order>
  </xsl:for-each>
</xsl:template>
```

As XML itself, XSLT leverages existing XML infrastructure

As you can see, XSLT is itself XML. So every XSLT document is also an XML document. Therefore, all of the tools for creating and managing XML documents work with XSLT documents. Of course, they do not necessarily understand the specific XSLT syntax, but they do provide some leverage. Although this example works with valid documents, XSLT works with well-formed ones as well. However, you would probably use XSLT when you had lots of documents in one data format that you wanted to translate to another data format—precisely the same conditions under which you would probably use DTDs.

XSLT enables the reformatting of data to meet specific requirements

XSLT is becoming an increasingly important part of the XML family of specifications. XML provides a general grammar for defining data formats, but as data moves through an organization, different consumers of the data will probably want it in different formats. XSLT provides the mechanism for supporting this customized data flow. It fundamentally alters the issue of information exchange from defining common data formats for all applications to defining the transformations necessary to deliver data to each application in the format it desires.

Overview of XML Schema

One of the latest XML-related initiatives is XML Schema. As the name implies, people intend to use it for specifying the structures of document types. DTDs already provide a mechanism for addressing this desire, but they have some drawbacks.

DTDs have some drawbacks

DTDs are the only part of the XML family of standards that do not themselves use XML document syntax. Therefore, applications and tools must be able to process both XML document and XML DTD syntax. Also, DTDs provide no mechanism for specifying the fundamental type of an element or attribute. Many people want to use XML as a universal data format for exchanging data, and not being able to validate automatically whether a value is an **int**, **float**, or **string** imposes an extra burden on the application programmer.

DTDs are not XML documents and lack datatyping

How It Works

Although it is perhaps slightly premature to begin developing applications with XML Schema, a simple example illustrates expressiveness not possible with DTDs. Example 3-8 consists of snippets of XML Schema code for the order document in Example 2-6. The first snippet shows how to define the "lineitems" element as a collection of 1 to 25 "lineitem" elements, illustrating more precise cardinality constraints than DTDs allow. Such constraints might be very important if, for instance, the order fulfillment system could handle only a maximum of 25 lineitems.

XML Schema has more precise cardinality constraints

*XML Schema
enforces datatypes*

The second snippet shows how to define the "State" element. In the United States, states have two-character identifiers. Therefore, Example 3-8 defines the "USAState" datatype and references it in the "State" element declaration. Not only can you enforce the string datatype, you can also enforce the number of characters. XML Schema includes pattern specifiers similar to the **COBOL** PICTURE syntax and regular expressions to constrain the format of content.

Example 3-8

```
<elementType name="lineitems">
  <all minOccur="1" maxOccur="25">
    <elementType name="lineitem">
      <any/>
    </elementType>
  </model>
</elemenTtype>
. . .
<dataType name="USAState">
  <basetype="string"/>
  <lexicalRepresentation>
    <lexical>AA</lexical>
  </lexicalRepresentation>
</dataType>
<elementType name="State">
  <datatypeRef name="USAState">
</elementType>
```

*XML Schema will
make data exchange
applications easier*

XML Schema has a number of other very useful features, such as the ability to define recurring blocks of elements or attributes once and then reuse this definition as often as needed. The timely release of XML Schema is a priority for the W3C. With its release, many existing data manipulation tools will integrate more smoothly with XML. Developing applications that exchange data will be much easier.

Technical Summary

❏ When a document contains elements generated by more than one author, Namespaces prevent collisions—order information from the Accounting and Fulfillment departments can be distinguished by "acct:order" and "ful:order," respectively.

❏ To avoid having namespace prefixes for every element and attribute name, the Namespace syntax allows authors to set the default namespace with the reserved "xmlns" attribute.

❏ XLink allows authors to link one XML document to another XML document or even to many other XML documents.

❏ XSL allows authors to present the content of the same XML document differently to two or more different audiences.

❏ When developers have two different DTDs that govern the same logical content, they can easily transform documents between the two formats using XSLT.

❏ Using XML Schema instead of DTDs to specify the content of XML documents offers the advantages of using XML syntax and enforcing datatype restrictions on element content and attribute values.

4

XML Tools

Executive Summary

As with any software technology, the availability of robust development tools to build an XML application is critical. Because XML is a
relatively new technology, you may have understandable concerns
about the availability and quality of these tools. Also, because people
want to apply XML to such a wide variety of applications, there is
opportunity for confusion over which tools may be appropriate.

Figure 4-1 presents a conceptual model of the relationships among
the major tool categories. As you can see, fundamental components
provide the foundation for the rest of the categories. Fundamental
components that support the XML specification are already widely
available from a number of large software vendors. The wide availability of these basic building blocks bodes well for XML support in
higher level tools.

Web infrastructure and development tools are rapidly maturing on
top of the solid base of fundamental components. By the beginning

*Development tools
are critical to success-
ful deployment*

*Fundamental com-
ponents are already
robust*

*Infrastructure and
development tools
are maturing*

**Figure 4-1: Relation-
ship of major tools**

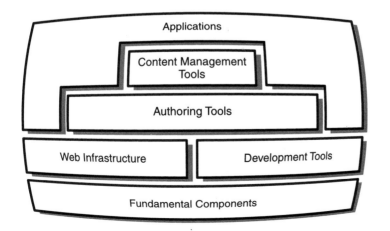

of 2000, all of the major Web infrastructure and application development tool vendors will have a high level of XML support in their products. The maturation of authoring tools and content management tools may take a little longer. Although many providers of such tools have adapted their existing offerings to support XML, it will take time for them to exploit fully all of its capabilities.

Support for related standards will soon emerge

The situation for the related standards discussed in Chapter 3 is somewhat different. Because most of these standards lag behind the XML specification in the standardization process, there is a corresponding lag in tool support for these standards. However, because most of these standards leverage XML, vendors can deliver support for them relatively quickly. Overall, the XML adoption rate for tool vendors is extremely high, so any delays in tool support will probably be less than for previous generations of software technologies.

Fundamental Components

Widespread adoption requires widely available components

The primary value proposition of XML is that it enables the spontaneous exchange of structured information. For such exchange to take place, all parties must be able to process XML documents. If they use related standards such as XLink, XSL, or XML Schema, they must be able to process that type of XML content as well. Therefore, a determining factor in XML's success is the availability of fundamental software components that provide such processing.

Major vendors provide XML components

Luckily, availability does not appear to be a problem. In many cases, fundamental XML components are becoming a standard part of operating systems and traditional application development tools. Powerful vendors such as IBM, Microsoft, and Sun were quick to offer XML *parsers*. As related standards become finalized, you can expect such companies to quickly offer components that support them as well. In addition to large vendors, there are a host of

smaller companies and free software organizations that provide
basic XML components.

For each of the XML family of standards you plan to use, you will
need a corresponding component. Chapter 3 already discussed
how these components work. Because the related standards are all
defined in terms of XML, they can leverage XML parsers. However,
we have not yet discussed how these parsers work.

*You need compo-
nents for each stan-
dard you want to use*

The most basic component of the XML paradigm is the parser. A
parser is typically embedded in an application. It reads in the physical files associated with a document and converts the document
text into programming constructs accessible to the application logic.
There are two basic types of parsers, tree based and event based.

*There are tree-based
and event-based
parsers*

Figure 4-2 shows the operation of a tree-based parser. It accepts an
XML document and an XML DTD. It then parses the document and
verifies that it follows the rules of the DTD. In the course of this

*Tree-based parsers
create a hierarchical
data structure*

**Figure 4-2: Opera-
tion of a tree-based
parser**

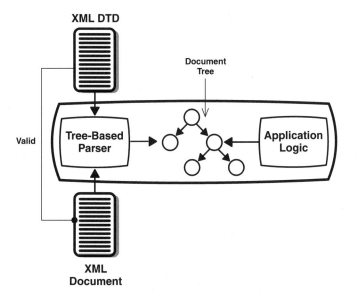

processing, it creates a hierarchical data structure that is the in-memory representation of the document tree.

Developers access the document tree through an API

The application logic accesses the hierarchical data structure through an **application programming interface (API)** provided by the parser. The Document Object Model (DOM) is another W3C Recommenation that defines the characteristics of the document tree and the API for manipulating it. A tree-based parser does not have to support DOM to support XML; it may have its own hierarchical data structure and API. However, DOM support is a good idea because it ensures that developers can learn one API and use any DOM-compliant parser rather than having to learn a new API for each parser. DOM and similar APIs allow developers to write application logic that moves through the document's tree of data, extracting and evaluating the information it requires to execute application functions.

The application can also create documents

This process can also work in reverse. The parser can read in a DTD and create a hierarchical data structure that serves as template for the application logic. The application logic can then use the API to create a new tree, add nodes to the tree, and fill them with data. The parser uses this newly created tree of data to create a corresponding XML document that conforms to the DTD. In this case, the application logic and parser work together as a document generator.

Event-based parsers require less memory

Tree-based parsers are highly effective for applications that need random access to document elements. However, building a complete tree for every document can be expensive in terms of memory. Event-based parsers avoid this cost because they do not create a data structure for the entire document.

Applications respond only to certain parsing events

Instead of creating a data structure and letting the application logic access it, event-based parsers send parsing events directly to the application logic. These events include the beginning and end of

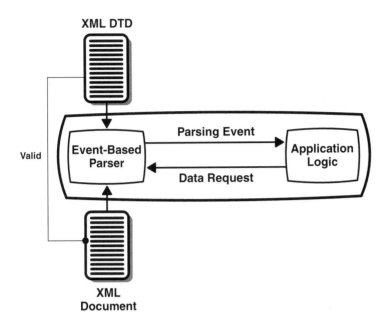

Figure 4-3: Operation of an event-based parser

each element but not its attributes or data. If the application logic is interested in that particular element, it requests additional data from the parser. This approach is highly effective when the application needs only sequential access to certain kinds of elements. Figure 4-3 shows how this process works with an XML document and DTD as input.

The *Simple API for XML* (SAX) is a commonly used event API for XML parsers. Example 4-1 illustrates the types of events a SAX-based parser would generate when parsing the order document in Example 2-6. As you can see, the parser does not include any element content or attribute information. When the application logic receives notification about the beginning of an element whose content it wants to access, it must specifically request information about that element.

Example 4-1

Start document
   Start element: addresses
      Start element: address
         Start element: firstname
         End element: firstname
         Start element: lastname
         End element: lastname

       . . .

      End element: address
      Start element: address

       . . .

      End element: address
   End element: addresses
   Start element: lineitems
      Start element: lineitem
         Start element: product
         End element: product
         Start element: quantity
         End element: quantity

       . . .

      End element: lineitem
      Start element: lineitem

       . . .

      End element: lineitem
   End element: lineitems

    . . .

End document

Parsers process well-formed as well as valid documents

Figures 4-2 and 4-3 show parsers accepting a DTD as input along with the XML document. In such cases, the parser validates the document against the rules specified in the DTD. Such parsers are called **_validating parsers_**. However, applications do not have to use the validating features of such parsers. There are also nonvalidating parsers designed for applications that require only well-formed documents.

Web Infrastructure

Although many XML applications may have nothing to do with traditional Web documents, support for XML on the Web is still extremely important to its achieving rapid adoption. Even though an application may not be directly Web related, it can still take advantage of XML-capable Web infrastructure. Microsoft has led the charge to support XML in its Web browser and servers. Expect the other leading vendors to add support rapidly in their infrastructure products as well. Figure 4-4 shows the Web infrastructure components and how they exchange XML documents. This infrastructure includes

Web support is important to the entire XML market

❏ **Web browsers.** The Web browser has become the default information viewing platform. For XML to achieve penetration

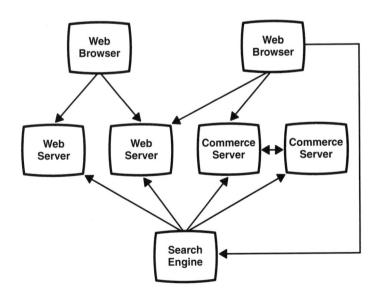

Figure 4-4: Web infrastructure components

as a structured information exchange technology, people must be able to view XML documents in their Web browsers. To enable such viewing, a browser must support XSL and include a number of default stylesheets that can handle any XML document. As you will see in Chapters 6 and 7, the ubiquitous availability of such browsers provides a great deal of leverage even to hard-core programmers using XML to build distributed protocols.

❏ **Web servers.** Two of the promises of XML are customizable presentation and improved Web searching. To deliver on these promises, Web servers need to do more than simply serve up documents with filenames that end in ".xml." For customized presentation, a Web server must have a means of communicating to clients the available presentations that it supports. For improved searching, the Web server must have a means of communicating to search engines the types of information it manages and the structure of that information. A sophisticated metadata interface could address both requirements. Another W3C Recommendation based on XML, *Resource Definition Framework* (RDF), provides just such a mechanism. For customized presentation, a Web server could use RDF to describe the set of XML document types it manages and the available presentations for each type. Based on a user profile, the browser could choose one of these presentations. For searching, a particular Web server might specify that it manages a collection of patent applications, that these patent applications are in XML, and their XML structure. The search engine could then proceed to use this information to create an index of the collection. Better yet, the server's RDF description could indicate the location of indexes that it already created.

❏ **Commerce servers.** Web commerce is rapidly becoming an enormous industry. There are two limitations of commerce technology that XML can help address. The first is helping consumers rapidly find products and services that interest them. The same RDF-based metadata interface that addresses the searching problem can address this one as well. A commerce server could provide a complete description of the types of products it offers and the structure of its catalog. Comparison shopping services and automated shopping agents could use this information to help customers find the lowest prices. The second limitation of traditional Web commerce technology is transaction complexity. Basically, most commerce is limited to simple buy-sell transactions between two parties using credit cards. However, there are many other transactions you might like to participate in. Ubiquitous support for XML-based standards for licensing intellectual property, multiparty transactions, and digital signatures enables a whole new level of Web commerce.

❑ **Search engines.** Support for XML in search engines is the converse of that outlined for Web and commerce servers. They must understand how to use metadata formats to find servers offering specific types of information and services, as well as discover the structure of that server's information and construct appropriate queries. These capabilities are very different from those of traditional text searching engines. Many companies are working on this new generation of technology, but there must be some simultaneous rollout of metadata-capable servers and search engines to deliver value to users.

XML can improve the existing Web environment with more flexible linking, customizable presentation, and improved searching. These advantages require server-side support for XML, XLink, XSL, and a metadata interface. Figure 4-5 shows how these features need to fit into existing server capabilities.

Delivering on XML's promises requires server support

Figure 4-5: Fitting
XML features into an
existing server

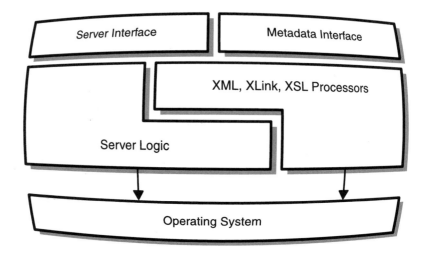

Figure 4-5: Fitting XML features into an existing server

Full support for the necessary features will take time

Under the hood, the server must include the fundamental XML, XLink, and XSL processing components. Developers must extend the server interface to enable clients to invoke the functionality in these components. They must also develop a new metadata interface to support search engines and client queries. Finally, they must integrate these new developments with the server logic so that these new features cooperate with existing ones. This upgrade process takes time, introducing a lag in infrastructure support for XML. Without a doubt, server vendors will eventually offer products with these capabilities, but you must be aware of the extent of the undertaking to predict delivery schedule and gauge vendor claims against reality.

Development Tools

Software developers need XML-capable tools

Many applications of XML concern the exchange of data between software applications. Some people believe that XML will become the *de facto* format for all tasks that require exchanging, managing, or storing structured data. Adding XML capability to this large population of applications requires a robust set of development tools. The most important ones include the following:

❏ **Document browsers.** Often, developers want to browse the content of a document as a tree, much as they browse class hierarchies or instance networks when developing object-oriented applications. They need an element browser that provides this functionality. In many cases, this browser consists of a stylesheet and Web browser that supports XML. However, developers manipulating XML from within traditional programming languages want support from within their **IDE**. Because providing such functionality is straightforward, many major IDEs, especially those for Java, will soon support this browsing.

❏ **Document manipulation libraries.** Applications that use XML as their primary data format must often extensively manipulate the documents they access. Conversely, they often have to construct documents on the basis of a complex set of internal conditions. Document manipulation libraries can simplify these tasks by providing high-level functions on top of fundamental components. Major vendors such as IBM, Microsoft, and Sun all have such libraries available or under development.

❏ **Data integration tools.** Many applications must map data from non-XML sources to XML formats. Developers need an efficient means of generating these mappings. Much like tools for mapping data from relational databases to object-oriented programming structures, these tools include features for browsing the structure of data sources and specifying which data to place in which elements. These tools can be very sophisticated because processing data from a non-XML source may require more than simply pulling data from a column and putting in an element. There may be datatype conversions or collapsing of relationships between tables. Many of the vendors of object-relational mapping tools have XML-relational tools under development.

❑ **DTD and Schema translators.** Many applications concern the exchange of information about coherent business entities. It is likely that different parties to these exchanges may have different definitions of these entities. In fact, given the suitability of XML for this problem, these different definitions will probably take the form of different DTDs or Schemas. As you saw in Chapter 3, XSLT can address this problem. However, for complex documents, it may be difficult and time consuming to create XSLT by hand. Creating a supply chain management system may require specifying translation for dozens of formats. Developers need higher level tools to make this process more rapid. The problem can be subtle and it may take some time for vendors to meet this need.

XML tools will come from existing tool vendors

XML affects a wide variety of different applications. Moreover, it doesn't really replace any existing technology. These factors make it necessary for XML to work side by side with many other software development technologies. Therefore, XML development tools must be integrated with existing development tools. Vendors of these existing tools must add support for XML or partner with specialists who build the solution for them. On the positive side, managers don't have to deal with many new, small vendors. On the negative side, inclusion of XML features may take these established companies a little longer to deliver.

Authoring Tools

Authoring includes both human and software document creation

To take advantage of XML's advantages for information exchange, people have to format information as XML documents. This authoring process includes both the hand coding of documents by humans and the automated generation of documents by software. Rapidly authoring XML documents requires support from the following types of tools.

❏ **Graphical DTD and Schema designers.** Designing DTDs
or Schema using a text editor can impede the productivity of
developers. A tool that enables them to focus on the information needs of users rather than syntax can speed deployment.
A graphical DTD or Schema designer works much like a data
modeling or computer aided software engineering (CASE)
tool. Designers use a palette to create visually the basic element structure of the DTD and dialog boxes to configure the
allowable element data and attributes. These tools are on
the horizon. The compatibility of Schema with the **SQL** data
model makes it likely that vendors of data modeling tools will
release Schema tools soon after the standard becomes finalized.

❏ **Document authoring tools.** Many XML applications
include static documents that human authors have to create.
Creating them with a text editor is a slow and error-prone
process. A document authoring tool allows an application
developer to create quickly a wizard- or form-based interface
that document authors can use to populate document
instances with data. Many of the initial applications of XML
have concerned the automated exchange of documents.
Hence, human authors have not yet become a visible bottle-
neck in the creation of XML documents. However, as their
participation increases, vendors will move to fill this need.

❏ **Stylesheet layout tools.** XSL is a highly sophisticated layout
description language. A large proportion of layout designers
with the necessary graphical design background to specify the
look and feel of stylesheets may not have the technical background necessary to create stylesheets by hand. Therefore,
they need stylesheet layout tools that allow them to configure
different page regions to display different types of elements
and specify the text format for element data based on rules
that operate on document content. These tools are coming
from vendors experienced with graphical user interface (GUI)

design tools such as IBM and Microsoft. Hard-core software developers typically use XML purely as a data format. Although they may not need fancy stylesheet tools because they view the documents only during troubleshooting or debugging, it is nevertheless a time sink for them to spend time creating stylesheets. They need tools that, given a high-level set of formatting preferences, can generate appropriate stylesheets for a DTD. Such tools will eventually be part of most IDEs that support XML.

❑ **Indexing tools.** A common requirement for applications that include static documents is allowing users to search through these documents. Indexing tools enable developers to create such lightweight search engines for their applications. The tool provides features for specifying how users may constrain element data and attribute values in their searches, creates the necessary indices, generates the search interface, and executes searches.

Vendors will offer different tools for different niches

To a great extent, existing Web tool and IDE vendors will provide these tools. Start-up companies that provide some of these components are emerging, but established vendors will probably consolidate the market through acquisitions and cooperative distribution agreements. In many cases, vendors may offer complete packages that include most or all of these tools. However, given the range of potential applications, these tools are likely to vary greatly in functionality and price. You need to make the appropriate trade-off between functionality and price for your particular applications.

Content Management Tools

As an organization adopts XML, more and more people within the
organization become involved in authoring XML content. As with
HTML and SGML, managing this content can pose a logistical challenge. Moreover, because many documents will be generated automatically by software, there is the possibility for new challenges and
even greater content volume. Figure 4-6 shows the general architecture of content management tools that can help address this
problem.

*Managing XML con-
tent is an issue*

Although vendors such as Inso and Interleaf offer complete content
management systems, the crossover between Web applications and
traditional software applications opens the door for new types of
content management systems based on databases and software
revision control systems. Also, large software companies such as

*Multiple vendors
provide solutions*

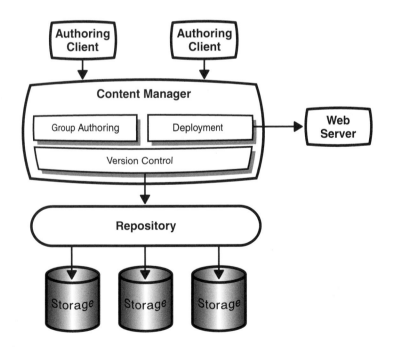

**Figure 4-6: Content
management tool
architecture**

IBM, Microsoft, and Oracle that have both database and development tools are looking at XML content management as a promising market. Whatever the source of the solution, it has the same basic components:

❏ **Repository.** The repository provides a robust and fault-tolerant location for storing XML documents, DTDs, and Schema. It consists of an interface that enables the content management system to store and retrieve information, a manager that controls physical storage, and the physical storage itself. The physical storage may be a filesystem, a relational database, or an object database.

❏ **Version control.** The version control component performs two functions. First, it prevents multiple authors from simultaneously making changes in the same content. Second, it maintains a version tree of all content. All requests to store or retrieve content must go through the version control system because it maintains the mapping of logical versions to physical data stored in the repository.

❏ **Deployment manager.** Upon instruction from an author, the deployment manager marshals a given version of content and publishes it to the appropriate delivery vehicle. In many cases, this delivery vehicle is a Web server. In that case, it must interface with the Web server to provide all the configuration information needed to serve the content.

❏ **Group authoring.** Although each authoring client has its own authoring tools, a content management system needs a component to coordinate the contributions of all authors. Typically, this coordination includes the maintenance of an authoring schedule and assignments for each author. It may also include real-time collaboration features that allow multiple authors to cooperate in creating a piece of content.

Although the XML paradigm has a great deal of flexibility because of its use of DTDs and separation of content from links and presentation, the same features exacerbate the content management problem. A given HTML page contains all content, links, and formatting instructions. The same content delivered as XML could have a document, a DTD, several external links, and several stylesheets. Synchronizing different versions of all these pieces almost requires a sophisticated environment.

The flexibility of XML contributes to the content management challenge

5

Processes and People

Executive Summary

As a manager, you will probably have at least some involvement in the project management and staffing of an XML application development effort. In most cases, the addition of XML to the technology mix will affect the project beyond simply requiring XML-related developer training and tool acquisition.

XML affects process and staffing

This impact depends on how much change will be required by your organization to develop the application. If your existing development processes and staff do not match those required, the cost of implementing the application will be particularly high. To estimate these requirements, we can categorize XML applications on the basis of their general intent:

The impact depends on the type of application

- ❏ **Content Documents.** Documents used primarily for the exchange of information among people.
- ❏ **Business Documents.** Documents representing business entities and intended for use by both people and applications.
- ❏ **Protocol Documents.** Documents used primarily for the exchange of information among applications.

Table 5-1 summarizes the development process and staffing requirements for each of the categories. The rest of this chapter analyzes the process and staffing requirements for each category in detail.

This chapter analyzes the impact by category

XML Applications Introduce Change

XML has potential benefits in almost every area of software development. However, most software development organizations do not have extensive experience with structured document technologies such as XML. In the past, the introduction of new software

You can plan ahead for XML's impact

Table 5-1: The development process and staffing requirements

	Content Documents	Business Documents	Protocol Documents
Resemblance to Existing Processses	Developing interactive Web site	Integrating business processes with software	Programming I/O portions of applications
Key Process Steps	• Stylesheet design • Repository integration	• DTD adoption • Backend integration	• DTD design • Application integration
Key Staff	• Producer • Information designer	• Standards bearer • Business analyst	• Protocol designer • Application developer

development technologies such as client-server architectures, object-oriented programming, and the Internet has resulted in significant disruptions to adopting organizations. You can mitigate this disruption by addressing the need for new processes and people prior to beginning the development of a production application. This strategy helps minimize the impact of XML on the software development process in three important areas:

❑ **Budgeting.** All software development organizations face a scarcity of resources. Therefore, you must efficiently allocate resources to application development projects and accurately estimate the cost impact of specification changes. New software development technologies usually have important effects on the cost of application development. For example, XML can reduce the cost of developing a given set of information exchange functionality. However, in addition to decreasing the cost of delivering currently envisioned features, XML can deliver completely new capabilities. But implementing such new features adds to the cost. New software development technologies also usually have an important impact on the timing of application development costs. For example, designing DTDs can increase the up-front costs of designing an application but can decrease the implementation and upgrade costs. Accounting for such impacts enables you to better allocate software development resources across an application's life cycle.

❏ **Staffing.** Using new software development technologies typically require new or different skills. For example, XML introduces the needs for developers able to design DTDs, manipulate the data structures produced by XML parsers, and create XSL stylesheets. Understanding the set of required skills allows you to make appropriate staffing decisions by finding new developers with these skills or providing these skills to existing developers through training programs.

❏ **Project Management.** Delivering an application on time and on budget requires the use of a software development process that matches the natural dependences in the application design. Such a process enables project managers to measure progress accurately and smoothly coordinate the need for different resources at different stages of the process. New software development technologies typically result in application designs with different types of dependences than previous technologies. For example, in many XML applications, the set of DTDs employed will drive much of the development work. However, much of the benefit from using DTDs comes from making them an explicit contract for interaction among several software applications. Therefore, DTD design often requires working with other software development organizations or at least taking their requirements into account. This cooperative process can often consume a considerable amount of time. But with DTDs in place, the work of document processing and stylesheet design proceeds more rapidly than you might otherwise expect. Acknowledging the need for process changes gives you the tools you need to keep the software development process on track.

Categorizing appli-
cations assists in
preparation

Clearly, the breadth of potential uses for XML means its effect on the software development process will vary greatly from project to project. However, by abstracting the similarities among XML applications into three categories, we can perform a high-level analysis of the software development process impacts. For each of these categories, this chapter examines two crucial areas:

❏ **Development process.** We examine the basic steps in the development process and the dependences among the steps. The particular steps provide a general framework for structuring timelines and budgets as well as revealing opportunities for parallel development. The steps presented include parts of the design phase and the entire implementation phase, ignoring the analysis, testing, and user acceptance phases. To a great extent, these other phases remain the same.

❏ **Required staff.** We examine the different types of staff and their required skills, tying their activities to the development process presented in the preceding section. Each type of staff has a label for convenience, although the actual employee titles will obviously vary from organization to organization. The important points are the roles of the different staff types and their respective skill sets.

Because there is a significant amount of variation among applications within each category, our analysis must apply generalizations. Clearly, the specific software development process for a particular application will deviate somewhat from the general model presented for the category to which it belongs. Moreover, differences among software development organizations will probably cause further deviations. However, the three general models can serve as guidelines that you can use to develop processes suitable for your particular applications.

Content Documents

In this application category, XML is something of a substitute for HTML. Usually, the document author wants to use XML over HTML for one of three reasons:

XML replaces HTML

❑ Users need the ability to search through a document archive using the metadata provided by XML tags. The search for works by William Shakespeare introduced in Chapter 1 is an excellent example. In this case, the document author wants to provide plays on line with the content marked up to indicate the role of each element. An online catalog is another example in which this type of search might be desired.

❑ The author wants to generate a large batch of documents electronically from an existing electronic source. Generating personalized news documents from news feeds and databases is an excellent example. In this case, the document author wants to define a common structure for all the documents and populate the structure automatically on the basis of certain parameters. An online football pool where the author wants to generate the results electronically for each user based on the user's individual picks is another example in which this electronic generation might be desired.

❑ Users need the ability to perform local processing on the document content. The home listing example introduced in Chapter 1 is an excellent example. In this case, the document author wants to allow users to download the document and process the data using a spreadsheet or analytical program. A home or automobile loan term sheet is another example in which this local processing might be desired.

People are the primary consumers of Content Documents. Software applications may index and search content documents, but the information within the documents themselves is meaningful

XSL is important because people are the target audience

primarily to people. It follows that presentation is important. Therefore, Content Document applications must heavily involve XSL stylesheets as well as XML documents, and sophisticated stylesheet creation tools must be available to deploy them.

Development Process

Application development is similar to Web development

Because Content Document applications often use XML to replace HTML, the development bears a certain resemblance to that of traditional Web applications. The primary differences lie in XML's cleaner separation of responsibilities between information design and presentation design. As Figure 5-1 shows, the development process for Content Document applications has the following seven steps:

❏ **Design DTDs.** The primary goal of most Content Document applications is to deliver structured information to human users. Therefore, the first step in the development process is assessing what information the users need and organizing this

Figure 5-1: The Content Document applications development process

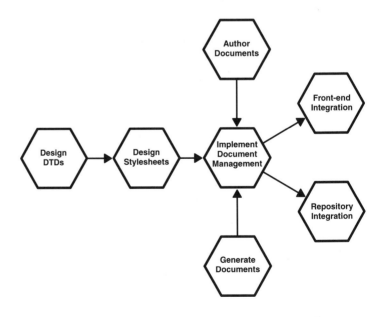

information as a set of DTDs. Because the information needs of users will vary from application to application, most Content Document applications will require custom DTDs. Application developers may be able to leverage some existing DTDs in whole or in part. However, because the value proposition of a new Content Document application is the delivery of information tailored to the needs of target users, custom DTD design will almost always be necessary.

❏ **Design stylesheets.** The primary target of Content Document applications is the human user. Human users process information most effectively when it is presented in a well-designed visual format. Therefore, once application developers have decided what information to present, the next step is to develop the layout for that information. In most Content Document applications, users will view documents within an XML-capable browser using stylesheets, so layout design implies stylesheet design. In some cases, users may require specialized client software for manipulating the documents. For such applications, layout design may imply more traditional graphical user interface design.

❏ **Implement document management.** The DTD design phase produces templates for the information delivered to users. The stylesheet design phase produces the layout for these templates. The next step is implementing the infrastructure necessary to marshal documents and stylesheets and then deliver them to users. This document management may be as simple as creating a filesystem directory with the appropriate permissions and configuring a Web server. It may include the use of a more sophisticated content management system to manage documents and the specification of additional information such as user-based customization instructions and security access controls.

❏ **Author documents.** With the document management infrastructure in place, the next step is providing the documents.

Many Content Document applications will include static XML documents. Human authors must create these documents. They may use rudimentary tools such as text editors or more sophisticated systems such as wizards that accept form-based input and then produce XML documents. For sophisticated authoring tools, developers will first have to acquire or develop them and then integrate them with the document management infrastructure.

❏ **Generate documents.** Many Content Document applications will include dynamic documents generated from data in external sources. For these documents, developers must establish a connection to the appropriate sources and specify the rules for generating documents from the data that they contain. Hopefully, developers will be able to use third-party tools for data integration to access the data sources. Otherwise, they may have to write custom code for this purpose. The rules for generating documents will operate on information the document management infrastructure elicits from users and may be implemented within a publishing tool or a scripting language.

❏ **Front-end integration.** After providing for the creation of the content documents, developers must provide for their delivery to users by integrating the application with front-end clients. For XML-capable Web browsers, this integration may consist simply of providing a link to a starting page from a well-known Web location. For non-XML-capable Web browsers, this integration will require distributing XML plug-ins or updated versions of the browser. For more sophisticated clients, developers may have to write custom code that connects the client graphical user interface to the document management infrastructure.

❏ **Repository integration.** In some cases, an application may require a long-term repository for content documents. Developers will have to integrate the document management infrastructure with the repository. An XML-specific repository will probably include automated functions for the storage and retrieval of XML documents. A generic repository will require writing custom code that stores and retrieves XML content using the repository's API. Note that repository integration can occur in parallel with front-end integration.

For very simple applications that deliver static documents via a Web server, the Content Document development process is nearly identical to the development of a traditional Web site. DTD design is the important new element. Developing applications that deliver dynamic XML documents via a Web server is very similar to developing dynamic Web applications with HTML. DTD design and the separation between designing stylesheets and generating documents are the important new elements. However, more complex applications with custom document management, nonbrowser clients, or use of sophisticated repositories add steps similar to those in traditional client-server software development.

Division of responsibility is the key difference

Required Staff

The similarities to traditional Web application development make the types of staff required for Content Document applications similar as well. As in Web applications, there is a split between authors of static documents and designers of dynamic documents. There is an additional split between information designers and presentation designers. Similarities also emerge in project management and support personnel. The following types of staff are required:

There is a split between information and presentation designers

❑ **Producer.** Whether for an intranet, extranet, or the Internet, Content Document applications must address the requirements of their target users. Because the target user groups are usually quite large and the expectations for responsiveness are usually quite high, there is a need for a type of staff dedicated to assessing user requirements continually and taking appropriate action—the producer. The role of the producer is to coordinate the identification of changes in user requirements with the allocation of resources necessary to implement appropriate application enhancements. During initial application development, the producer plays much the same role as a traditional project manager, determining application goals, and managing the development schedule. However, appealing to thousands of users and making daily changes requires a more dynamic ongoing role similar to that of a producer in the media industry. The producer will have experience in project management and product development or design.

❑ **Information designer.** Content Document applications deliver information to human users. The information designer, taking direction from the producer, determines what information to provide and how to organize it. This staff type participates primarily in the DTD design phase. However, the information designer may also participate in the implement document management and repository integration phases. These phases require the information designer's input on the probable usage patterns of the different document types so that other types of staff members may implement efficient document management infrastructure and repository access. The information designer will have experience in requirements gathering, requirements specification, and data modeling.

❑ **Layout designer.** The layout designer develops the stylesheets and, if necessary, the graphical user interfaces for the application. These designs depend on the types of documents designed by the information designer and the information gathered about users. In some cases, the producer will arrange user focus groups in which the layout designer participates to gather this data. The layout designer will have experience in graphic design, Web page design, and perhaps user interface design.

❏ **Application developer.** Sophisticated Content Document applications may require the coding of custom software. These applications require an application developer. The role of this staff type is to supply programming expertise for the creation of custom document management infrastructure, custom document authoring tools, and custom document generation tools. The application developer will have expertise in appropriate programming languages such as Java and Perl.

❏ **Document author.** Document authors have domain-specific knowledge that they need to encode as XML documents. To facilitate the rapid capture of this knowledge, they should use wizard-based authoring tools, although they could use text-based templates. They will have expertise in the particular domain for which the application provides content.

❏ **Data integrator.** For applications that generate documents from external sources, the data integrator translates the information format in the sources into the appropriate DTD format. In some cases, this translation may simply require using a graphical tool. In others, it may require some scripting. The data integrator will have experience in database programming or administration and perhaps programming languages such as Java and Perl.

❏ **Administrator.** The administrator is responsible for configuring the document management infrastructure, for instance Web servers, and ensuring the ongoing operation of the application. This includes the application hardware, the document management infrastructure, the authoring system, the generation system, and the repository. Sophisticated applications may require more than one administrator. The administrator will have experience as a Webmaster, system administrator, perhaps as a network administrator, and perhaps as a database administrator.

*Information design-
ers are the hardest
slot to fill*

When compared with the staff for traditional Web applications, the information designer is probably the most revolutionary addition to the development team. The separation of information format design from presentation design and document authoring makes explicit a role fulfilled implicitly by a number of different traditional staff types. The combination of general requirements gathering skills and specific DTD design skills is likely to be the most difficult to find. In the short term, layout designers, application developers, data integrators, and repository integrators with XML technology experience may be in short supply, but their skills will be transferable enough to make learning XML relatively straightforward.

Business Documents

*Humans and soft-
ware can use the
same format*

In this application category, XML documents contain information about fundamental business entities such as customer, order, and invoice. The crucial benefit of XML is that it allows humans and software to use these documents in the same format. The need for Business Document applications usually stems from one of three requirements:

❑ **Automate the workflow of document processing.**
Everyone agrees that moving paper documents around is an efficient means of executing business processes. However, prior to XML, automating workflow had two drawbacks: (1) businesspeople were tied to a particular workflow system and (2) the document representation often violated business people's concepts of what a document looks like. With XML Business Documents, all workflow systems that can process XML can interoperate and businesspeople are free to view actual documents while the system is free to process the underlying data.

❑ **Synthesize actual documents from business software systems.** Typically, business systems present business information in terms of its underlying data model. Often, this representation is not particularly convenient for businesspeople, especially when a logical business document encompasses information from multiple business systems. Software engineers who build these applications do not want to hand-create each type of document. Synthesizing XML Business Documents using an automated tool is an efficient solution for both parties.

❑ **Automated document exchange.** With the connectivity enable by the Internet, many businesses want to achieve operational efficiency by automatically exchanging Business Documents over the Internet. XML Business Documents such as Order and Invoice constitute the seed of an effective supply chain management system. Each business simply needs to accept the definition of the Business Documents and map them to representations in business software systems. Software engineers do not have to hand code a translation bridge between every company and businesspeople can still view the documents if they wish.

The strength of Business Document applications is that people can view documents and software applications can process them using the same underlying representation. Presentation concerns are significant, so XSL plays a certain role in these applications. Businesspeople want to view the documents in an understandable layout, but the need for visual sophistication is less than that for Content Documents. On the other hand, software engineers need sophisticated tools for mapping XML element hierarchies to the data models used by business software applications.

XSL and sophisticated development tools are required

**Figure 5-2: The
Business Document
applications develop-
ment process**

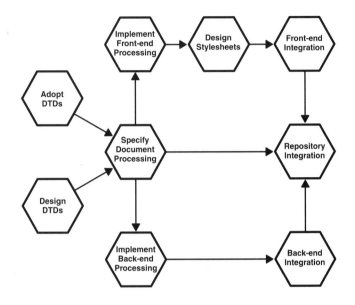

Development Process

*Combine business
modeling with soft-
ware development*

In some sense, Business Document applications differ the most
from traditional software development. Their general goals are to
provide a means of universally defining common business concepts and provide the infrastructure for cooperatively manipulating
these concepts. At the analysis level, some organizations have used
information engineering or **business object modeling** to
define common business concepts in a fashion analogous to XML
DTD design. But even then, they actually implement the information exchange based on these models on an *ad hoc* basis. XML provides a means of formalizing the implementation of more general
information exchange services. As Figure 5-2 shows, the development process for Business Document applications has the following
nine steps:

❏ **Adopt DTDs.** Because Business Document applications concern the exchange of information related to fundamental
   business concepts, there are often existing DTDs for these con-

cepts. In some cases, industry groups may propose a set of DTDs to cover common business concepts. In others, a partner may want to agree on common DTDs. In yet others, a vendor of a third-party software package may provide DTDs. In all these cases, application developers have three choices in how they adopt DTDs. One, they may simply adopt the DTDs. Two, they may work with the other parties to help define the DTDs. Three, they may choose to use parts of the DTDs but extend them to meet their particular needs.

❏ **Design DTDs.** In some cases, Business Document application developers may need to define fundamental business concepts that are unique to their organization or develop enhanced definitions that give their organization a competitive advantage. In these cases, application developers will design their own DTDs.

❏ **Specify document processing.** Because Business Document applications typically reflect one or more business processes, they must include rules for document processing that reflect the business process rules. For example, in workflow applications, these rules will reflect the path that business documents may take. In information aggregation applications, these rules will reflect how to aggregate source information to add value.

❏ **Implement front-end processing.** Business Document applications have human users. Developers must therefore implement the document processing rules that apply to the documents produced and consumed by human users. These rules may include allowable actions such as "approving" or "rejecting." They may also include security restrictions. Developers must develop or acquire the code necessary to enforce such rules.

❏ **Design stylesheets.** Human users comprise one of the target audiences for Business Document applications. Human users process information most effectively when it is presented in a well-designed visual format. Therefore, once application developers have decided what information to present and the processing rules that apply to the information, the next step is to develop the layout for that information. In some Business Document applications, users will view documents within an XML-capable browser using stylesheets, so layout design implies stylesheet design. In other cases, users may require specialized client software for manipulating the documents. For such applications, layout design may imply more traditional graphical user interface design.

❑ **Front-end integration.** With the front-end processing rules and interface layouts in place, developers must integrate them with front-end clients. For XML-capable Web browsers, this integration may consist simply of providing a link to a starting page from a well-known Web location. For non-XML-capable Web browsers, this integration will require distributing updated versions of the browser or XML plug-ins. For more sophisticated clients, developers may have to write custom code that connects the client graphical user interface to the front-end processing implementation.

❑ **Implement back-end processing.** Software users comprise the other target audience for Business Document applications. Developers must therefore implement the document processing rules that apply to the documents produced and consumed by software users. These may include required actions such as "update" or "place order" as well as transaction restrictions. Developers must develop or acquire the code necessary to enforce such rules. Note that this step and the next step may occur in parallel with the previous three front-end steps.

❑ **Back-end integration.** With the back-end processing rules and interface layouts in place, developers must integrate them with back-end systems. Developers must establish an interface to these systems and implement the code necessary to propagate the processing rules through these interfaces. Developers should be able to use third-party tools that dynamically synthesize XML documents from data stored in enterprise data sources. Otherwise, they may have to write custom code for this purpose.

❏ **Repository integration.** In some cases, an application may require a long-term repository for business documents. Developers will have to integrate the document management infrastructure with the repository. An XML-specific repository will probably include automated functions for the storage and retrieval of XML documents. A generic repository will require writing custom code that stores and retrieves XML content using the repository's API. Note that repository integration can occur in parallel with front-end and back-end steps.

A principal characteristic of Business Document application development is that developers must address the needs of both human and software users. Therefore, after an initial set of steps necessary to agree on a set of information exchange formats, the development process really has two separate paths, one for the human users and one for the software users.

Paths correspond to human and software users

This situation contrasts with traditional software development, where there are constraints from either human or software users but not both. The existence of constraints from both sources can have negative schedule effects in a spiral development process. Although the two branches of development may occur in parallel, once one branch has feedback that requires changes in the DTD or document processing phases, the feedback affects the other branch, potentially setting off another round of feedback. Achieving the benefits of parallel development therefore requires excellent up-front design to minimize midstream changes.

Feedback between paths can slow development

Required Staff

Success requires a particularly wide range of skills

Because the goal of Business Document applications is to align information exchange with business process flow, implementing such applications requires a wide variety of staff types. Skills have to include business partnership management, business process analysis, and developing interfaces for the different components of the enterprise information architecture. Specific types of required staff include the following:

❑ **Standards bearer.** Because Business Document applications deal with the exchange of information about fundamental business entities, standards bodies are likely to take a strong role in defining DTDs describing these entities. Logically, a standards body may be an accredited standards organization. It may also be an industry group or even an internal group within a large enterprise. In any case, the application development organization needs a person to represent the organization on the standards body. This standards bearer will ensure that DTDs describe business entities in a way that meets the needs of the organization. The standards bearer will need a combination of both business and technical experience. This experience may include line of business management, business process design, and application design.

❑ **Business analyst.** The business analyst's role is to make sure that the DTDs defining business entities and the document processing rules accurately reflect the organization's business processes. The analyst will collaborate with the standards bearer to define the organization's goals for the standards body and will collaborate with the architect to decide which DTDs to adopt and how to design internal DTDs. The business analyst will have experience in line of business operation, business process design, and perhaps data modeling.

❏ **Architect.** Most Business Document applications will span a large user population and a large number of back-end systems. Therefore, there is a need for a staff member to coordinate a large spectrum of technical design tasks. The architect will work with the business analyst to specify DTDs and document processing rules and will work with application developers, user interface designers, and the different integrators to ensure that the application architecture will work within the constraints imposed by their respective components of the application. The architect will require a wide variety of technical skills including requirements analysis, application design, and data modeling.

❏ **Application developer.** In some cases, the development of a Business Document application will require the development of code to implement unique business logic. In workflow applications, there is the workflow engine to implement. In information aggregation applications, there is the aggregation engine to implement. These tasks require an application developer with experience in the appropriate programming languages and tools.

❏ **User interface designer.** For the parts of a Business Document application that interact with human users, there is a need for appropriate user interfaces. A user interface designer specializes in designing such interfaces based on how the information to be presented relates to the user's job task. This staff type has a number of options for the design including the use of stylesheets, special browser plug-ins, and custom clients. Of course, these choices will be constrained by the overall architecture of the application. The user interface designer will have experience in user requirements analysis, graphic design, Web page design, and user interface design.

❏ **Client integrator.** In many cases, the user interface will need integration with the existing client infrastructure. This integration may include the deployment of updated browsers, the deployment of special plug-ins, and the deployment of custom user interface clients. For plug-ins and custom clients, there may be issues of integration with client desktop management and configuration tools. These tasks are all the purview of the client integrator, who will have skills primarily in browser configuration and desktop management.

❏ **Data integrator.** Because a Business Document application must provide for the exchange of information with existing applications and data sources, there is the crucial problem of integrating the Business Document application with these existing systems. The data integrator translates the information format in the sources into the appropriate DTD format. In some cases, this translation may simply require using a graphical tool. In others, it may require some scripting. The data integrator will have experience in database programming or administration and perhaps programming languages such as Java and Perl or the APIs of particular packaged applications.

❏ **Repository integrator.** Implementing the repository integration step in the software development process may require the installation and configuration of the repository as well as custom programming if the repository does not already supply appropriate XML-ready interfaces. The repository integrator is responsible for these tasks. This individual will have expertise in database design and database administration and preferably experience with the particular repository.

Coordinating staff from different backgrounds presents a challenge

To a great extent, all the staff types required to deploy Business Document applications already exist within many enterprises and vendors. The problem is that they rarely have to coordinate their actions to the extent necessary with XML. Of course, much of this lack of coordination stems from the fact that standards bearers, business analysts, application developers, interface designers, and data integrators do not have a common basis for communication. A unique benefit of XML is that it can provide this common basis. However, project managers still have to address the problem of co-ordinating and facilitating communication among these separate types of staff.

Protocol Documents

In this application category, XML documents serve as the data encoding framework for protocols. For the purposes of categorization, we use "protocol" in the broadest sense—a set of allowable actions and a set of corresponding message formats that allow two software applications to exchange data. There are opportunities to create new classes of Internet applications to solve specialized problems. Electronic software distribution (ESD), in which customers install a software program from the Internet instead of from a CD-ROM, is one example. Remote help desks, where a technical support representative remotely diagnoses problems with a computer's software configuration, is another.

XML serves as the data encoding mechanism

In both of these cases, two computers have to exchange a series of messages over the Internet or through a filesystem to accomplish the task. One of the barriers to implementing such protocols is agreeing on message formats. XML DTDs provide a straightforward method of formally defining the format for a message. Another implementation barrier is building the software to encode and decode these messages and forward the resulting data to the main application for processing. By using publicly available XML engines, software developers can avoid writing much of this code themselves and, more important, are much less likely to discover errors in the encoding-decoding logic because a publicly available engine has probably undergone far more testing than is possible for a custom engine.

DTDs define message formats

Engineers may use
XSL for debugging

Software applications are the primary consumers of Protocol Documents. You could define a basic XSL stylesheet for each message type so that software engineers could view messages in a format convenient for debugging. Engineers get this feature essentially free. However, it is a secondary concern when compared with the leverage they get from using off-the-shelf technology. Of course, a key requirement for achieving this benefit is access to publicly available and commercial grade XML engines, as well as the tools for rapidly integrating them with applications written in different programming languages.

Development Process

XML is tightly
integrated with
applications

Protocol Document applications bear a certain resemblance to the components of applications that manage input/output with the filesystem or over a network. The primary differences lie in the generalization of the information formats that XML allows. Moreover, the nature of Protocol Document applications makes them only one component of a larger application. They serve as the engine that enables information exchange; the higher level application performs all the application-specific information processing. As Figure 5-3 shows, the development process for Protocol Document applications has the following five steps:

❑ **Adopt DTDs.** Because the primary goal of Protocol Document applications is to enable the exchange of information between different software applications, software developers do not usually have the luxury of designing all the DTDs themselves. Most of the time, they want to exchange information either with an application that already uses particular DTDs or with an application whose developers want to have input into the DTD design process. In the first case, the application developers simply adopt the DTDs used by the target applications. In the second case, they must work with either a

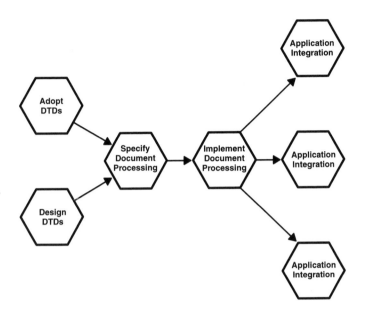

formal standards body or an informal cooperative group to
agree on a mutually acceptable set of DTDs.

❏ **Design DTDs.** In some cases, Protocol Document application
developers may control all application components that will
exchange information. In others, their application may provide a natural focal point in a group of cooperating applications whose developers are looking for leadership in the
specification of DTDs. In these cases, Protocol Document
application developers may design the necessary DTDs by
themselves.

❏ **Specify document processing.** Because Protocol Document
applications are essentially components of higher level applications, developers must specify how the Protocol Document
component interacts with higher level applications. This specification may simply be an API. It may also include a set of
utilities for manipulating the information contained in the
protocol documents to facilitate processing by higher level
applications. For applications that use the filesystem to ex-

change documents, this document processing specification will include any conventions for directory and file use. For applications that use the network to exchange documents, this specification will include the messaging and network protocols as well as the allowable order of document exchange.

❏ **Implement document processing.** Generally, because different applications will communicate using Protocol Documents, there will be room for different implementations of the document processing specification. Therefore, application developers must either acquire a third-party implementation or develop one on their own.

❏ **Application integration.** Once developers have a Protocol Document component, they must integrate it with the higher level application. This integration will consist of using the component's API and utilities. Some applications will use them to extract the information from protocol documents and integrate it with the data structures used by the higher level application. Others will use them to take information from these higher level application structures and encode them as Protocol Documents.

Tools and libraries provide a great deal of leverage

Both enterprise and vendor developers may use third-party tools and thereby skip all but the last step. These tools will probably take care of mapping interchange data to application data, but developers may have to write some custom integration code. In some cases, developers may be able to acquire complete protocol engines. Then they need simply integrate the higher level application logic with the protocol engine through its APIs. Of course, enabling developers to avoid all but the last step means that some vendor has completed the first four steps.

Traditional application developers play a key role

Required Staff

Because the development process for a Protocol Document application essentially boils down to the design of the protocol and the use

of the protocol within different applications, the required staff boil
down to those who participate in protocol development and those
who use the protocol within different applications. The types of
protocol development staff are the interesting additions. There are
three types of protocol development staff in addition to the application developers who actually use the protocol in their respective
applications.

❑ **Standards bearer.** As noted in the discussion on the Protocol
Document application development process, developing Protocol Document components will often require cooperation
with other parties that plan to use the protocol. This cooperation may take place through a formal standards body, an
industry group, or informal meetings. In any case, the application development organization needs a person to represent
the organization in the cooperative development process. This
standards bearer will ensure that the protocol DTD meets the
needs of the organization and that its future development
plans coincide with the future development plans of the other
participating organizations. The standards bearer will have a
significant amount of development experience, including
architectural design as well as experience cooperating with
outside parties.

❑ **Protocol designer.** If the Protocol Document application uses
custom DTDs, the protocol designer will need to design these
DTDs. Whether the protocol DTDs come from within the software development organization or from an outside organization, the protocol designer will have to specify the document
processing. The role will include designing the Protocol Document component APIs and specifying appropriate abstraction
layers to allow replacement of messaging and network protocols as well as future extension of the component. The protocol designer will have experience in application design, API
design, and data format design.

❏ **Library developer.** Each organization using a protocol will need an implementation of a corresponding Protocol Document component. During the document processing implementation phase, the library developer will write the code that implements the protocol, services API calls, and provides utilities. This implementation will need an appropriate level of abstraction so that different higher level applications can use the library and that application developers can swap the library out for a different implementation. The library developer will have experience implementing libraries in the necessary language such as C, C++, or Java.

❏ **Application developer.** The point of Protocol Document components is that developers of higher level applications can use them to enable their applications to exchange information. Therefore, for any given Protocol Document application, there may be many higher level application developers who have to integrate the corresponding component into their applications. These developers will have ownership of the corresponding development tasks for their applications and experience in the same language as the Protocol Document component's API.

XML leverages an existing set of skills

None of the staff types required to implement Protocol Document applications are new. Protocol design has long been a recognized area of software development expertise. However, standards bearers, protocol designers, and library developers will have to translate this expertise to XML. In most cases, the learning process should proceed quickly because self-describing protocol message formats such as ASN.1 and s-expressions have long been a part of protocol design and implementation.

Application Spectrum

In using the categorization to estimate the impact of XML on your organization, you must remember that Content Documents, Business Documents, and Protocol Documents are convenient labels. Of course, XML applications fall across a continuous spectrum, with these labels applying to regions of the spectrum. Clearly, there are certain applications that have some characteristics of Content Documents and some of Business Documents. Others have some characteristics of Business Documents and some of Protocol Documents. It's rather difficult to imagine an application with some characteristics of Content Documents and some of Protocol Documents. Figure 5-4 shows that this spectrum has four interesting dimensions.

Applications actually fall across a spectrum

Humans are the principal consumers of Content Documents. Software applications are the principal consumers of Protocol Documents. The defining characteristic of Business Documents is that they have both humans and applications as principal consumers.

Human versus software parties

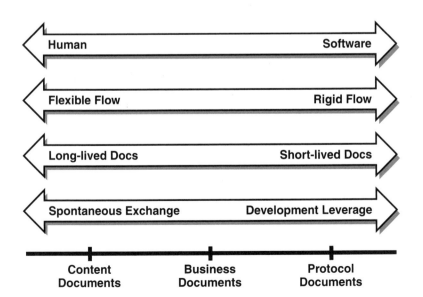

Figure 5-4: Four dimensions of XML documents

The extent to which your application has human and application users determines to what extent you will experience the impacts associated with each of the three categories.

Flexible versus rigid flow

Who consumes XML documents is a fundamental application characteristic, but it is highly correlated with flexibility or rigidity of the document flow. The document flow characteristic is the allowable order in which a consumer may process documents. Not surprisingly, human document consumers desire the capability for flexible flow. They want to move from document to document without constraint as it serves their particular purpose or even their whim of the moment. On the other hand, software application consumers require rigid flow. They do not have the capability to handle arbitrary documents in arbitrary order. Where both humans and software applications consume documents, humans must accept more rigidity and software applications must have the capability to handle more flexibility. It is usually within a particular domain such as finance, manufacturing, or telecommunication that this compromise is possible. The domain provides the boundaries that make more rigid flow acceptable to humans and the collective information resources necessary to make more flexible flow possible for software applications. The relative flexibility or rigidity of the flow of your application determines the extent to which you need information designers or protocol designers.

Humans desire spontaneous exchange

A more subtle correlation with the nature of document consumers is the motivation for using XML in the first place. With human consumers, a primary motivator is the ability to conduct spontaneous exchange. XML provides the foundation by which two parties that do not have a prior agreement can exchange information. With an XML DTD, they can unambiguously agree on the relationships of different elements. With XSL stylesheets, they can view the information according to their own preferences without affecting the underlying information. With XLink links, they can relate documents without having to get permission to modify the documents themselves. The goal is to decouple the document author from the document consumer. Each consumer can extract structured information from documents created by different authors. Each author can present structured information to many different consumers.

With software application consumers, a primary motivator is the development leverage that XML provides. Because XML is a standard mechanism for describing document structure and then formatting documents, a lot of software code is available for encoding and decoding XML. By using XML, software developers avoid having to develop this code themselves. Moreover, they know that by using XML, they open up their information exchange to other software application with little effort. They can avoid much of the effort spent defining and implementing programming interfaces that others can use. They simply make the appropriate DTDs publicly available. The relative desire for spontaneous exchange or leverage in your application determines the extent to which you develop using an interactive media model or a traditional software model.

Developers desire leverage

6

Five XML Applications for Enterprises

Executive Summary

The best way to understand the potential for XML is to consider some examples. Such consideration should provide inspiration in how to use the technology in your organization. Table 6-1 lists five examples of important enterprise applications where XML can deliver significant benefits. The rest of this chapter discusses these applications in detail.

This chapter presents enterprise examples of XML applications

Table 6-1: Enterprise applications and XML benefits

Application	Category	Examples	Key XML Benefit
Information Distribution	Content Documents	• Partner coordination • Project mgmt	Delivery of structured data that target audience can manipulate
Knowledge Management	Content Documents	• Product planning • Technical support	Extensible knowledge structuring and wrapping of existing documents
Workflow	Business Documents	• Purchasing • Expense reports	Portable process specifications and standard interfaces to business applications
Application Integration	Business Documents	• Supply chain mgmt • ERP/HR integration	Portable business entity definitions and infrastructure for format translation
Data Integration	Business Documents	• Customer mgmt • Product information mgmt	Customized data formats and document synthesis from data sources

Enterprise Application Types

An enterprise application uses XML to provide an *operating benefit* by increasing the efficiency of business process execution or enabling new business processes. The rest of this chapter presents

XML can deliver operating benefits to enterprises

five applications where XML offers a siginificant advantage in delivering an important operating benefit. For some of these applications, enterprise software developers themselves do not create software that manipulates XML documents. In these cases, third-party software provides these capabilities. However, there are product selection, installation, integration, administration, and extensibility issues that require the enterprise to understand how the underlying XML features work.

Information Distribution

Business Challenge

Information distribution is a competitive advantage

As information becomes a greater share of the value added in producing products and delivering services, information distribution capabilities become a more important component of enterprise competitiveness. Enterprises need to distribute information internally to employees, externally to partners and customers, and generally to the public. The Web has been successful as an enterprise computing technology because it provides an effective information distribution channel.

HTML can be cumbersome

Although HTML documents have had a great deal of success, they do have certain drawbacks. In cases where the primary value of documents is in the dynamically retrieved data they contain or where users want to manipulate information locally, HTML is cumbersome.

XML Benefit

XML is more efficient for delivering dynamic content

There are a number of Web technologies that embed dynamically retrieved data in Web pages. The need for these technologies stems from the fact that HTML is a page layout language and putting data in these pages requires altering the text of the HTML document sent to the browser. The combination of XML and XSL is a much more efficient solution. The XML paradigm keeps the information separate from the presentation rules, giving the enterprise a great many more options such as performing presentation processing on either the server or client and allowing the client to apply personal preferences to the presentation.

Because the information and presentation rules remain separate, human users can manipulate information locally by importing it into a spreadsheet or dragging it and dropping it from browser to spreadsheet. Software applications can directly access the information by ignoring the stylesheets altogether. This capability makes XML a true information distribution technology rather than a page publishing technology.

XML preserves the logical structure of data

Architecture

As Figure 6-1 shows, the information distribution architecture is very similar to the typical Web server architecture. Clients request documents from the Web server. The Web server retrieves the corresponding XML document and appropriate stylesheet from their respective repositories and returns them to the client. In cases where browsers do not support XML, the server could preprocess

This application is similar to traditional Web applications

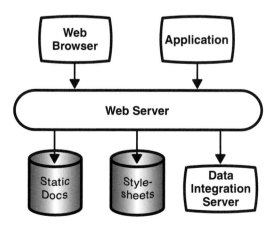

Figure 6-1: The information distribution architecture

the XML document and stylesheet to create a server-side HTML document. Typically, XML browser clients process the document and stylesheet themselves, although they may choose to substitute local stylesheets for the ones retrieved from the server. Application clients would usually ignore the stylesheet completely and simply process the XML document directly.

There can be static and dynamic documents

There are two potential types of XML documents, static documents and dynamic documents. Static documents reside in a repository. Repositories may be filesystems or content managers. Dynamic documents can be synthesized using a data integration server, discussed later in this chapter. In this case, clients submit XML documents containing the parameters of dynamic requests. The Web server forwards these parameters to the data integration server, which assembles the required XML documents from data stored in back-end data sources.

Key Features

Web server delivery is a key feature

A key feature of this application type is that a Web server distributes the XML documents. A distinguishing feature is that it allows for static XML documents created by human authors as well as dynamic documents created by software applications.

Development Process

You identify the desired information and create DTDs

You develop an information distribution application in XML much the way you develop traditional dynamic Web applications. First, you must identify the types of documents to distribute and create the appropriate templates. In this case, a template consists of a DTD and one or more stylesheets. For static documents, human authors use authoring tools to create the documents. For dynamic documents, you use a data integration server to create them. The simplicity of this development process is what makes XML a compelling information distribution technology.

In some cases, vendors may provide complete systems for distributing certain types of information such as product catalogs and specifications. In this case, you are responsible for authoring any static documents and integrating the third-party solution with any of your applications that it uses as a data source for creating dynamic documents.

For some applications, vendors may provide a complete XML solution

DTD Source

When you create your own information distribution system, your developers create all the DTDs. When you use a vendor's product, the vendor would supply the DTDs. In many cases, XML will provide an integration benefit by allowing enterprise developers and many different vendors to use the same infrastructure to distribute different types of information based on their respective DTDs.

XML streamlines integration of custom and packaged solutions

Document Life Cycle

Human authors create static documents and store them in a repository. Static documents reside in the repository until explicitly destroyed. A data integration server creates dynamic documents and passes them to the Web server. They will be implicitly destroyed once sent to a client unless explicitly archived. Of course, clients may choose to do anything they want with the documents. If an information distribution application includes a large number of static documents or archives a large number of dynamic documents, it will require a sophisticated content document management system to store and retrieve these documents.

Static documents persist, dynamic documents don't

Knowledge Management

Business Challenge

For many enterprises, their greatest assets are the accumulated knowledge of their employees. Unfortunately, these assets reside primarily in the brains of these employees, making the assets difficult

These applications help leverage knowledge assets

to control and leverage. To achieve greater control and leverage, many enterprises turn to knowledge management systems. These systems attempt to catalog important areas of knowledge and make them available to employees throughout the enterprise. Technical support, problem diagnosis and repair, and product design are all areas where knowledge management can decrease costs or increase revenues by making the experience of key employees available to the entire organization.

XML Benefit

XML helps structure knowledge

There are three fundamental problems in knowledge management: (1) modeling knowledge, (2) leveraging existing documents, and (3) searching the knowledge base. XML includes facilities that address each of these areas. Having random bits of knowledge floating around the enterprise is not particularly useful. Therefore, enterprises want a structured way of modeling knowledge. XML DTDs provide a convenient mechanism. For a given type of knowledge such as home accounting software problem diagnosis, airplane engine troubleshooting, or semiconductor manufacturing process design, the enterprise would define a DTD that specifies and structures the important elements of that type of knowledge.

XML can add knowledge information to existing documents

Problem (2) in knowledge management stems from the fact most enterprises have large volumes of existing documents that contain knowledge. What they need is a means of adding information to these documents that describes the knowledge they contain. With XML, you can create a wrapper document type that includes metadata about the document and an XLink to the document.

XML tags facilitate searching

Problem (3) in knowledge management is searching the knowledge base. Because XML is highly structured, searching is not a problem. In fact, by tagging each piece of information with its contextual meaning or wrapping existing information with XML metadata, using XML enables the automated analysis of the knowledge base by software agents, making it possible to inform employees pro- actively of knowledge relevant to their jobs.

Architecture

As Figure 6-2 shows, a knowledge management system comprises a knowledge manager, knowledge sources, and stylesheets for pre- sentation. A knowledge source may be a knowledge document that is a self-contained description of an area of knowledge. It may also be the combination of a wrapper document that provides metadata about a non-XML document and that source document.

The knowledge man- ager brokers access to knowledge sources

When an employee has an experience and wants to enter it into the knowledge base, the employee requests the appropriate form from the knowledge manager. *Extensible Forms Description Language* (XFDL), is an XML-based format for describing forms and is a possi- ble forms solution. In this case, the form would capture all of the

Employees enter knowledge with forms

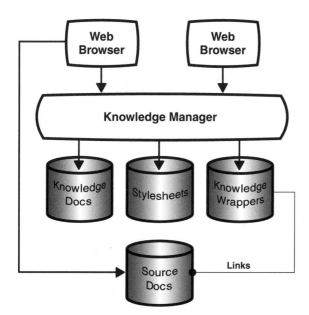

Figure 6-2: The knowledge manage- ment architecture

information necessary to populate the corresponding knowledge document. Using a Web browser capable of displaying and processing XML documents, the employee enters the appropriate information and submits the document to the knowledge manager. The knowledge manager processes the form and creates the knowledge document.

Employees or agents catalog existing documents

To make existing documents available as part of the knowledge base, there are two possible techniques. Employees can enter wrapper information using forms, the same way they would enter a direct experience. Automated agents can also scan the source documents and create wrapper documents. The attractiveness of the automated option depends on how effectively the agent can generate metadata from the document content. If the document contains structured information such as an entry in a sales contact database, the process may be very effective. If the document is unstructured text, it will probably not be.

The knowledge manager provides search and notification services

As knowledge and wrapper documents enter the system, the knowledge manager indexes them and stores them in the knowledge base. Through their Web browsers, employees can query the knowledge base for help with any problem type supported by the system. They view the knowledge documents using the stylesheets appropriate for each DTD. To view the source documents linked to wrapper documents, they of course require the appropriate applications for viewing those documents. Employees may also register interest in types of knowledge and the manager may then proactively inform employees through e-mail when such knowledge becomes available.

Development Process

You would probably buy a knowledge management system

You are most likely to evaluate, select, and purchase a knowledge management system from a vendor. Given the sophistication of knowledge cataloging techniques, it's unlikely that you would build your own knowledge management system from scratch. However, you may very well use XML to customize and extend a third-party product.

In either case, you need DTDs that categorize the types of knowledge managed by the system. Designing DTDs for knowledge categorization is much more difficult than for workflow applications, discussed subsequently. With workflow, the business process is observable. With knowledge categorization the internal problem solving process of the employees is not observable. Therefore, you need specially skilled knowledge engineers to assist in the DTD definition process. A companion task to designing DTDs is designing the stylesheets that employees will use to view knowledge documents. Because employees from different organizations may access the same knowledge, you may need multiple stylesheets for each DTD to provide customized presentations to employees using the knowledge for different job tasks. Because effectively imparting knowledge requires effectively presenting knowledge, stylesheet design is a crucial part of the development process.

Knowledge engineers design DTDs

Once you have the DTDs, you have to get knowledge into the system. Perhaps the biggest challenge is getting employees to spend time entering knowledge or creating wrappers. Achieving this goal may require an extensive education campaign and special incentives. With the knowledge in the system, there may be some minor education necessary to teach users the best ways to use the system to assist in the performance of their jobs. However, given that they will use their Web browsers to access the system, the amount of education should be minimal.

Convincing people to enter knowledge is a challenge

Key Features

A distinguishing characteristic of knowledge management compared with traditional Web publishing systems is the fact that users,

The single author many readers model is a key feature

as opposed to designated document authors, input most of the information in the system. Also, for any given document, there is an asymmetry to the relationship between creator and consumer; a single person creates each document and many people may consume it. Another important characteristic is that document consumers always find relevant documents through the knowledge manager as opposed to directly accessing them.

DTD Source

Most knowledge DTDs require customization

In many cases, knowledge engineers will either extend existing DTDs or create DTDs from scratch. In certain specific applications, such as software technical support, third-party vendors may be able to create DTDs that are general enough to apply to many enterprises.

Document Life Cycle

All knowledge documents persist

Either enterprise employees or automated agents provide the data for the knowledge manager to create documents. Enterprise employees who need assistance from the knowledge base consume these documents. In marked contrast to the other enterprise XML application types, all documents remain alive. The entire point of knowledge management is to accumulate information, so destroying documents does not make sense. Therefore, the knowledge management system must include a document repository capable of handling very large volumes of data.

Workflow

Business Challenge

Workflow systems streamline business processes

There are many enterprise business processes that require human staff and software applications to process information in a series of well-defined steps. Typically, each actor in a business process path acts upon a work product and sends it to the next actor in the path.

Purchase authorization is a relatively simple example. Strategic enterprise planning is a complex one. To eliminate the inefficiencies of paper documents and *ad hoc* access to software applications, many enterprises have turned to workflow systems to manage such business processes.

Using a business process design tool, a business analyst defines the work product, the actors, and the allowable actions at each step. The workflow system then shepherds the work product from actor to actor, enforcing the policies specified in the business process design.

The workflow system enforces the business process rules

Traditional workflow systems require special client software. For human actors, the use of special software imposes both learning and ownership costs. For software actors, the need for translation between the workflow API and the software's native API imposes software development and maintenance costs. Moreover, as enterprise business processes become more sophisticated, they begin to include more and more subprocesses from different organizations within the enterprise. If these organizations use different workflow systems, there is a potentially enormous integration barrier to achieving smooth process flow.

Traditional workflow systems have high adoption costs

XML Benefit

XML can address all three of these challenges. Standard components of the enterprise desktop such as e-mail clients and Web browsers are beginning to gain XML capabilities. Therefore, human actors can use these familiar desktop applications as their interface to the workflow system, decreasing learning and ownership costs.

Browser clients reduce user costs

XML is also gaining acceptance as an integration technology. Later in the chapter, we'll look at the use of XML for application integration. Therefore, it is likely that workflow systems based on XML

Widespread support for XML reduces integration costs

will be able to leverage integration tools also based on XML, decreasing software development and maintenance costs.

Process interchange
formats ensure com-
patibility

Finally, efforts to provide XML-based workflow standards will ensure that different workflow systems can exchange business process descriptions. Not only does such interoperation decrease integration costs, it also enables enterprises to use different workflow systems for different tasks, based on their particular strengths, without sacrificing the ability to manage cross-functional process flow.

Architecture

Systems support human
and software actors

As Figure 6-3 shows, a workflow system may connect to multiple human and software actors. Human actors usually access the sys-

**Figure 6-3: The
workflow architecture**

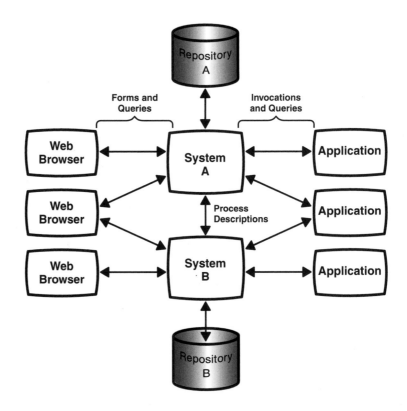

tem through e-mail clients or Web browsers. In some cases, e-mail clients or browsers may need special plug-ins or other extensions so that they can operate on work products. Software actors interact with the system either through native XML interfaces or mediated through XML-based integration tools.

XML work products flow in both directions between actors and the system. If more than one system exists, work products may also flow between them. Each system must maintain a repository of all work products in process. It is possible, although not necessary, that two or more systems may use the same repository.

Documents flow in both directions

In addition to moving work products to and from actors, a work-flow system may initiate contact with actors to check on the status of work products or alert them to important events. Actors may initiate contact with the system to query the status of work products assigned to other actors, ask for summary reports, and register interest in important events. In fact, *Simple Workflow Access Protocol* (SWAP) is an XML-based mechanism for performing these tasks.

Actors may query the system for status

Key Features

The most prominent feature of workflow systems is that the documents sent from manager to actor are the same documents sent back to the manager by the actor. Each document defines a work product. When the manager sends one to an actor, the document lacks information that the actor must supply. When the actor send it back to the manager, it is the same document with the missing information added. This mode of exchange is logically different from most client-server exchanges, where the request has a completely separate ancestry from the reply.

The same document instances flow in both directions

Development Process

In most cases, you will buy a workflow system

The first step in the development process is to select, purchase, and install a workflow system from a third-party vendor. Of course, in rare cases, you may decide to build your own workflow system from scratch.

You specify the process and connect the actors to the system

Once the system is installed, you must configure it to manage each business process. The first step is defining the work products for the business process. Each work product consists of one or more DTDs. The next step is defining the actors participating in the business process. For human actors, you may have to define an XSL stylesheet for each DTD to control the presentation of that type of document. For software actors, you have to integrate the work-flow API with the software application's native API. The last step is defining paths among the actors and the allowable actions at each step. For a purchase authorization process, the workflow system may check to see if the purchase request is over a certain amount, sending it to a vice-president if it is, at which time the vice-president may either decline or approve it.

DTD Source

Off-the-shelf DTDs work for adminis-trative processes

Because business processes differ greatly from enterprise to enter-prise, it might seem as if an enterprise would have to define its DTDs from scratch. However, in many cases, the actual work prod-ucts for a business process may be the same across enterprises, it's only the business process paths that are different. For example, travel expense reimbursement forms include essentially the same information in every enterprise. The expense amount thresholds triggering the need for managerial approval and the type of approval necessary may vary. Therefore, for administrative business processes, DTDs may come completely from third parties.

In other cases, the work products may be substantially similar across enterprises but with minor differences. Third parties can therefore provide basic DTDs that enterprises may customize. A special version of this situation arises when an industry consortium defines a set of DTDs for a set of common industry business processes. The third party in this case is the consortium, but the enterprises who will use the DTDs contribute to the design process.

Consortiums may provide foundation DTDs

Certain business processes will be unique to a particular enterprise. In fact, part of the benefit of workflow systems is that they allow enterprises to adapt business processes rapidly to changing business conditions. Therefore, enterprises that use workflow systems almost certainly have to design at least some of the DTDs corresponding to work products. The workflow system should include tools to make this process easier than editing DTDs by hand.

Value-added processes usually require custom DTDs

Document Life Cycle

Business events outside the workflow system typically trigger the creation of documents. An employee returning from a business trip would trigger the creation of a travel expense reimbursement document. A customer placing an order would trigger the creation of several documents related to order processing. The passage of time would trigger the creation of several documents related to end-of-year accounting.

Business events trigger the beginning of a process

Once a document is created, there is a difference between the logical and physical document life cycles at this point. Logically, the same document receives updated information at each step in the business process. Physically, there may be two versions of the document: the one before update and the one after update. Logically, at the end of the business process, there is a single document that represents a finished work product. Physically, there is a set of documents representing the preupdate state of the work product

Physically, there may be multiple versions of a document

at each step in the business process. The set of physical documents represents the ancestry of the logical document.

Not all processes require audit trails

This distinction is important for maintaining audit trails. For certain business processes, an enterprise may not care about the intermediate states of the logical document, only the final state. In these cases, the physical version would cease to exist after an updated version becomes available. In other cases, the enterprise may want to maintain an audit trail for legal or policy reasons. Then the workflow manager would save versions of some or all physical ancestors for a given logical document.

Application Integration

Business Challenge

Business process automation requires application integration

Many enterprises have turned to packaged applications as a solution to rapidly automating business processes. Packaged applications typically support a finite range of business processes, so most enterprises use more than one packaged application. However, to increase efficiency further through automation, enterprises must integrate these packaged applications with each other and with custom application. Typically, achieving such integration requires extensive custom consulting or expensive tools.

XML Benefit

Standard XML formats for business entities enable smooth integration

Although not a canned solution, XML provides the foundation for simplifying this process. XML includes the infrastructure for inputting and outputting documents containing metadata. If applications could agree on a set of XML document formats for common business entities and transactions, they could work together. The Open Applications Group has developed just such a set of formats and a number of leading packaged application vendors such as Oracle, Peoplesoft, and SAP plan to support them.

Moreover, once applications included this basic functionality, they would have fundamental XML components embedded. They could then leverage these components by enabling the mapping of customized XML formats to application formats. This evolution would greatly reduce the cost of application integration.

It is not far from supporting standard formats to supporting custom formats

Architecture

As Figure 6-4 shows, the application integration architecture includes one or more applications communicating over a network. When one application wants to access another application, it sends it a standard XML-formatted request. The target application returns an XML-formatted business document. Note that a set of document formats is not sufficient to enable communication. There must be an exchange protocol. Client and server applications must agree on how to establish a network connection, for instance, using HTTP over port 5500.

Applications make requests and return results as XML applications

The applications shown in Figure 6-4 do not have to be in the same enterprise. You could just as easily integrate an Inventory Management application in one enterprise with an Order Fulfillment application in another enterprise. When inventory falls below a certain level for a given part, the Inventory Management application sends

Application integration can cross enterprise boundaries

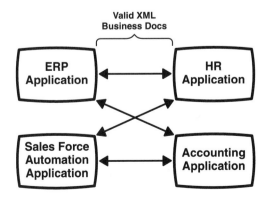

Valid XML
Business Docs

Figure 6-4: The application integration architecture

an XML document over the Internet to the Order Fulfillment application at the part supplier. The definition of XML formats for business entities and transactions has the potential to simplify greatly the development of supply chain management applications.

Key Features

Integration documents are meaningful to people

Application integration is a particularly interesting XML application. Document exchange occurs primarily between applications. However, the documents they exchange represent business entities and transactions. Usually, when two applications exchange documents, these documents are primarily interesting only to the applications themselves. But many application integration applications would be perfectly meaningful to business professionals, once formatted with an XSL stylesheet.

Development Process

You may have to add XML support to internally developed applications

In most cases, packaged application vendors provide support for XML. In these cases, you must test all the applications in question to ensure that they can exchange information using the exchange protocol. In some cases, you may need to enhance internally developed applications so that they can communicate with other applications using XML. In these cases, you have two primary tasks. First, you create a protocol engine that can format a document request, establish a remote connection to the server application, send the document request to the server, receive the server's response, and extract the interchange document. Second, you create a mapping layer that will translate the data contained in the interchange document into data structures that the application can process.

DTD Source

Industry standards groups will supply many DTDs

Because application integration commonly occurs between operational enterprise applications, enterprises with similar operations have similar interchange requirements. Therefore, consortiums within particular industries such as financial services, semiconductor manufacturing, or telecommunications are defining DTDs and interchange protocols.

Document Life Cycle

An application creates a document in response to a specific request. It then returns the document to the requesting application, which consumes it by translating the information contained in the document into internal data structures. At this point, the document no longer exists unless explicitly saved for archival.

Documents are temporary

Data Integration

Business Challenge

Unfortunately, the information constituting logically coherent business concepts such as vendor, customer, product, order, and invoice often resides in several different data sources. This information diffusion causes two problems: (1) enterprise staff find it difficult to execute job functions that require them to assemble a complete representation of such business concepts and (2) each application must incur the performance cost of assembling the component data into complete representations of such business concepts.

Desired information often resides in multiple databases

XML Benefit

An obvious solution to this problem is centralizing the process of synthesizing component data. Unfortunately, whatever service performs this synthesis must provide the resulting information in a format that might itself turn out to be incompatible with that used by other systems in the enterprise. XML can address this issue. Because Web browsers have become a standard component of the enterprise desktop and next-generation browsers will support XML, there is a strong argument for using XML as the universal data format for human clients. Also, because many of the business-to-business

XML can become the de facto data format

commerce solutions currently in development can process XML documents, there is a strong argument for using XML as the universal data format for software clients. The widespread availability of XML-capable clients and its flexibility in structuring information make it possible for XML to become the *de facto* data format.

Architecture

The server composes documents from back-end data

As Figure 6-5 shows, the architecture for data integration includes one or more data sources, a data integration server, and one or more types of clients. The data sources could include files in a filesystem, databases, and applications—anything with remotely accessible information. The data integration server takes data record components from these sources, composes them into XML documents, and makes them available to clients. It also accepts updated documents from clients, disassembles them into their component information elements, and instructs the data sources to change the corresponding component data records. The data integration server

Figure 6-5: The data integration architecture

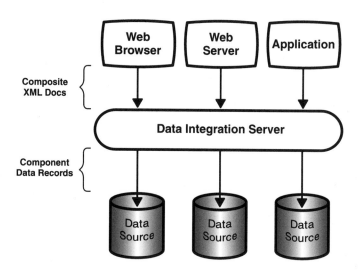

does not have to use an XML-based mechanism to access and update the information sources. It could also use native database APIs, **JDBC**, or **ODBC**.

A client may be an application that processes data from multiple sources. It could also be a Web server that then passes the documents on to end users. End users could even use XML-capable browsers to access the data integration server directly.

Clients may be applications, Web servers, or browsers

Key Features

The true middleman nature of the data integration—it only assembles information; it does not use it as part of a business process—helps distinguish it from other applications. The fact that it does not necessarily use XML documents as the means of exchange with information sources is also an important characteristic.

The lack of document processing is a key feature

Development Process

In nearly all cases, you will purchase a data integration tool from a vendor. A number of smaller vendors such as Bluestone, Data-Channel, and Object Design have begun offering such tools. Larger vendors are considering offering their own products. After selecting a synthesis tool, there are two important steps in implementing a synthesis application: (1) figuring out what types of business information human and software users need supplied and (2) locating the component data.

You will probably buy a data integration server

Step (1) is a needs assessment problem. You identify all the different groups that want synthesized information and explore the needs of each. Then you design a set of DTDs or Schema that meet these needs. Once you know what data you need, you move on to step (2). Step (2) is a data access problem. Find out which data sources contain the required data and gain access to those sources.

Identify the required data and locate the data sources where it resides

You map component data to element content

With DTDs in hand and access to the component data, you map the elements and attributes specified in the DTDs to data fields in information sources. The vendor should supply a tool for browsing the schema of information sources and then creating the necessary mappings. However, you may have to specify a number of important parameters such as concurrency policy, transaction policy, and access control policy. Finally, you test the system to make sure the mapping works and the parameters specified produce the expected behavior.

DTD Source

If you want to synthesize information to meet the needs of internal users, you create a DTD for each business concept that you want to make available. If you want to integrate back-end information sources so that they can exchange information with systems already using a specific XML document format, the DTD will come from whoever designed those particular systems.

Document Life Cycle

Documents are temporary unless cached

The data integration server creates XML documents based on the requirements of clients. In most cases, it may create these documents dynamically for each request. The document would be destroyed as far as the data integration server was concerned as soon as it was sent to a client, although the client might retain one or more copies. As part of the middle tier, the data integration server may also choose to cache documents.

7

Five XML Applications for Vendors

Executive Summary

Vendors of software products and services have their own opportunities to take advantage of XML. Examples help illustrate these opportunities and help provide inspiration in how to use the technology in your organization. Table 7-1 lists five examples of important enterprise applications in which XML can deliver significant benefits. The rest of this chapter discusses these applications in detail.

This chapter presents vendor examples of XML applications

Table 7-1: Enterprise applications and XML benefits

	Category	Examples	Key XML Benefit
Personalized Web Sites	Content Documents	• Portals • Online shopping	Portable user profile definition and flexible content customization
Information Aggregation	Business Documents	• PC component info • Academic research	Easy format translation and document assembly
Software Bill of Materials	Protocol Documents	• Automated upgrades • Desktop management	Ability to interpret configuration across products
Configuration and Logging Files	Protocol Documents	• Component deployment • Security logs	Compatibility of development and analysis tools across software implementations
Distributed Protocols	Protocol Documents	• Component deployment • Security logs	Faster development through access to standard formatting infrastructure

Vendor Application Types

A vendor application uses XML to provide a *selling benefit* by reducing the cost of delivering existing product features or enabling new product features. This chapter looks at the selling benefits for five

Vendors achieve a selling benefit with XML

applications interesting to vendors of software products and services. The first two applications apply primarily to vendors of Internet services and concern XML benefits that make certain service features easier to develop and more robust. The last three applications apply primarily to vendors of products and concern XML benefits that make certain software features easier to develop and use.

Customized Publishing

Business Challenge

Customization builds viewership

A common Internet business model is generating advertising revenues by attracting viewers with information services. Viewer retention is a difficult problem, and many Internet services are finding that publishing information customized to the needs of each viewer helps build viewership.

HTML customization technologies are limited

Current technologies for dynamically generating HTML have some drawbacks. They are typically suitable when there are a few well-defined custom pieces of content. As the level of customization increases and Internet services attempt to customize the structure of information, these technologies either fail utterly or become very expensive to maintain. Furthermore, the level of customized presentation is fairly rudimentary.

XML Benefit

XML offers more flexibility and smoother integration

Because XML is designed to manage structured information, it is easy to substitute different content for different users within a given structure and create structures customized for different users. Also, the desire of enterprises to use XML as an integration technology benefits Internet services. Much of the information necessary to publish customized content resides in systems similar to those that enterprises plan to integrate using application or data integration. Therefore, there is an economy of scale in using XML as the means of incorporating customized information.

There is an additional cost advantage. A challenge with HTML technologies is separating the software development process from the content development process. Because the customization essentially occurs through embedded software code, these two processes are horribly intertwined, making it difficult for service producers to gauge the impact of rolling out additional customization features. XML enables a clear separation of responsibilities. Presentation specialists design stylesheets. Viewer product specialists design the DTDs that govern the type and structure of information available. Source integration specialists provide the integration with the sources that contain the information.

XML enables a clear separation of responsibilities

Architecture

As shown in Figure 7-1, clients access the customized publishing system through the Web. The Web server identifies the customer through standard Web mechanisms and passes the identity to the

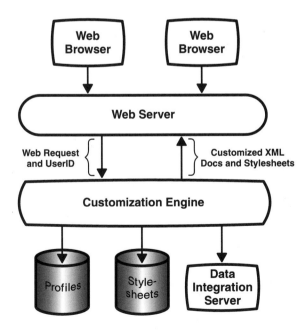

Figure 7-1: The customized publishing architecture

customization engine. The customization engine decides what information to present to the user and what stylesheets to include based on an XML-formatted profile. On the basis of the profile retrieved, the customization engine decides which DTD to use and pulls this information from the appropriate back-end sources. It also selects the appropriate stylesheet from the stylesheet repository and returns it along with the document.

Key Features

Customized Web interaction is the key feature

The key features of customized publishing are the Web-based interaction with human users and the complete customization of the information delivered.

Development Process

Eventually, vendors will supply complete customization solutions

Third-party vendors supply some application components. At a minimum, third parties supply stylesheet authoring tools, the Web server, and the data integration server. Eventually, most services will probably also use third-party customization engines, although leading-edge Internet services such as the major portals may well build their own.

Profile design is an important success factor

Successful customization depends on effective profile definition. You must create a DTD for describing the kinds of preferences users may have and the actions the engine can take based on those preferences. Preferences certainly include presentation desires such as "large fonts," "16 colors," and "bullet points." They also include the parameters necessary to instruct back-end sources which information to provide a particular user. Example 7-1 shows a possible set of parameters in an XML format.

Example 7-1

```
<interests>
  <sport>
```

```
    <league>NCAAMensBasketball</league>
    <team>Stanford</team>
  </sport>
  <sport>
    <league>NFLFootball</league>
    <team>Denver</team>
    <team>Minnesota</team>
  </sport>
</interests>
```

A particularly strong advantage of using XML for Web experience customization is the potential for combining preferences from different sites. The more information you have about a user, the better you can customize the user's experience. If you partner with several different Internet service providers that use XML-based profiles, you can easily pool this information.

Service providers can pool their XML profiles

Whether you build your own customization engine or buy one from a third party, you still have the problem of implementing the publishing solution. The first step is to identify target users and gather data on the types of information they want and the points of customization that are important. User programming specialists then encode this user model in the preference framework and create the necessary DTD and stylesheet options. Screen designers create a set of style options for each DTD. Data integrators then use a data integration server to map the information in the back-end sources to the elements defined in the DTDs.

User requirements fuel DTD and stylesheet design

DTD Source

To a great extent, the structure of the information is the Internet service's competitive advantage. Therefore, you will probably want to design your own DTDs for content. You may well design your own profile DTD, but joining forces with a group of service

Design your own content, but cooperate on profiles

providers could deliver more benefit, because the more information you have about users, the better you can anticipate their needs.

Document Life Cycle

Profiles are persistent, customized content is not

The customization engine creates content documents from information stored in back-end sources. Users consume these documents via the Web server. Unless explicitly preserved, these documents are destroyed upon consumption. The whole point of customized publishing is to provide a unique experience based on the most current information available, so it is unlikely that you would preserve these documents. On the other hand, the point of the user profile is to maintain preference information, so you would definitely preserve it.

Information Aggregation

Business Challenge

Information aggregators are the Internet equivalent of distributors

Value-added resellers have become an accepted source for products and services. They provide a valuable function by aggregating the components of various vendors into a complete solution for particular organizations or individuals. Information aggregators are the digital equivalent of value-added resellers. They take pieces of information from a number of different sources and aggregate them into packages of information customized for particular organizations or individuals.

An aggregator may facilitate the flow of goods

In some cases, the aggregated information may facilitate the flow of physical goods and services. Consider the problem of PC configuration. Thousands of vendors sell components for PCs. Millions of customers want to order PCs with combinations of these components. How can these customers be sure that the combinations of components they order will work together? They certainly don't want to sort through all the product specifications for each component they may want. Information aggregators provide the solution. To a certain extent, PC retailers act as the information aggregators and guide customers in the selection of compatible components. However, the sheer volume of component combinations and the rate at which available components change are too great even for most retailers. An independent information aggregator could address this problem by gathering information from all the component vendors and organizing it so that retailers and customers can access it to determine workable configurations of PC components. *RosettaNet* is a PC industry effort aimed at using XML to address this issue.

In other cases, an aggregator may add value to information that is already valuable. Consider the problem of scientific research. Thousands of papers are published each year on a wide variety of topics. Thousands of experiments generate terabytes of data. Most of this information is spread across hundreds of different research organizations. An aggregator could take the information from all the available sources and make it available to researchers. These researchers could then generate new information based on this access and contribute it back to the aggregator.

Aggregators may add value to pure information

XML Benefit

There are two barriers to efficient information aggregation: one on the input side and one on the output side. On the input side, the problem is that the information component suppliers have a wide variety of different sources, each with its own format. Extracting the desired information in a machine-readable format is an onerous task that isn't cost justified in any but the most critical areas. On the output side, the problem is ensuring that the potential information consumers can effectively use the aggregated information in the format supplied.

Proprietary formats restrict information aggregation

DTDs themselves become valuable information

Not only can XML address both barriers by providing common formats, it introduces an additional value added—DTD design. By designing DTDs that capture the essential features of information components in the particular domain, you help information suppliers make their information more valuable. By designing DTDs that capture the information requirements of information consumers, you gain a competitive advantage. Essentially, you create value by making the market for information efficient.

XSL and XLink provide additional leverage

Not only do XML DTDs provide a convenient mechanism for you to streamline the flow of information, XML also provides other essential infrastructure for free. Information consumers certainly want to view the aggregated information. XSL stylesheets provide the ideal means. Not only can they view the information with their Web browsers, but also stylesheets can be quickly customized to the needs of different types of information consumers. An important aspect of organizing information is indicating relationships between different pieces. XLink provides a convenient way to specify such relationships independent of the actual information. Your only service could be creating XLinks that represented a package of documents.

Architecture

Gathering and publishing information are logically separate

Figure 7-2 shows the architecture for a potential XML application. A gatherer process accesses the XML documents from each information provider. It then processes the documents, performing whatever processing and aggregation are necessary. It is this processing and aggregation that constitute the unique value. The gatherer then stores the resulting documents in a repository. In response to client queries, a publisher process accesses the appropriate documents in the repository, combines them with the appropriate stylesheets, and sends them to the client. Of course, the

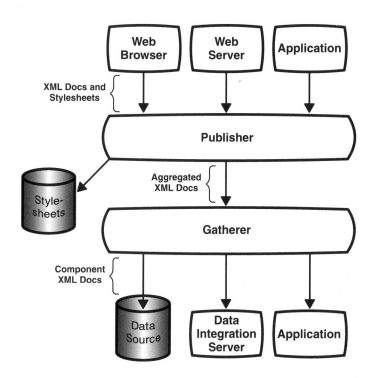

Figure 7-2: The information aggregation architecture

gatherer and publisher may be part of the same software exe-
cutable; however, there is a certain logical separation to their functions. A given information provider may supply more than one
information aggregation application and clients may query information from more than one information aggregator.

Key Features

The key feature of information aggregation is the flow of documents from information supplier, to information aggregator, to
information consumer. At each step, the information aggregator
provides value—first by extracting only the relevant information
from the information supplier and then by responding to particular
client queries.

*Creating an infor-
mation food chain is
a key feature*

Development Process

Mapping supplier resources to consumer desires creates value

To start the development of an information aggregation application, there are three critical design tasks. First, you have to figure out what information consumers think is valuable. This process results in DTDs for the document types consumers will download from the aggregator and accompanying XSL stylesheets. Second, you have to figure out what information suppliers have that the you can use to build the information that consumers want. This process results in DTDs for the document types suppliers will upload. Third, you have to figure out precisely how to generate the information consumers want from the information that suppliers provide.

Supplier data may not be in XML formats

After the design phase, you need to provide access to consumer clients and achieve access to supplier sources. A Web server is probably the easiest way to provide access to clients, although there are other possibilities such as e-mail. A Web server is also the easiest way to achieve access to sources. Unfortunately, the reality is that most suppliers have information in existing systems and need to use a data integration server to provide the documents. You may well have to build this application yourself if suppliers are unwilling to bear the cost.

DTD Source

You provide the DTDs

You probably want to design the DTDs yourself. However, industry standards could exist for certain types of information from suppliers, in which case you could leverage these existing DTDs. You probably want to try to get suppliers to adopt your DTDs as an industry standard.

Document Life Cycle

Aggregated documents are persistent

Information suppliers create and maintain their own documents. They may choose to maintain their documents in a repository or dynamically generate them from back-end sources. Gatherer processes consume these documents and, from them, publisher processes create their own documents. You definitely maintain these documents in a repository because they are your primary assets. Information consumers consume these documents and potentially archive them at their own sites.

Software Bill of Materials

Business Challenge

Most commercial software applications have an installation program that selects the precise files that it will place on the machine and configure any operating system or application preference files. As many such developers have learned, it is a good idea to create a software bill of materials (BOM) file that contains this information and put it on the machine as well. Then, when a new version of the application becomes available, an installer can intelligently upgrade the machine based on the contents of this BOM file. Moreover, the existence of such BOM files makes it possible for third-party tools to catalog and analyze the software installed on a machine for reasons such as automated upgrades over the Internet and desktop software management.

Maintaining software configuration information is critical

XML Benefit

There are three principal requirements for the BOM file: (1) easy to create, (2) easy for humans to view, and (3) easy for software to process. Using standard off-the-shelf XML parsers to create XML-based BOM files addresses requirement (1). Providing an XSL stylesheet that enables users and administrators to view the installation configuration quickly with their Web browsers addresses (2). Saving the file in a format that any other software developer can access easily with an off-the-shelf XML parser and the appro-

Using XML eliminates proprietary formats

priate DTD location addresses (3). Using XML as the BOM file format decreases development time and increases the openness of the application.

Architecture

The installer creates the BOM file

As Figure 7-3 shows, the application installer is the primary actor in BOM creation. It analyzes the existing configuration of the machine and prompts the user for any necessary information. From this data, it decides how to configure the application installation. It then puts the appropriate files on disk and updates any applicable preference files. It also saves the configuration information as an XML document. Later, an upgrade tool, desktop application management tool, or even another installer can access the BOM.

Key Features

The meaning of the BOM is the key feature

The key feature of an XML-based BOM is that the XML document represents the configuration of a software application installation.

Figure 7-3: Using a software BOM in the installation process

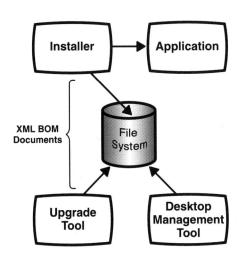

Development Process

The development process for an XML-based BOM is very simple. The installation program will already have a set of decisions it can make when installing the application. You simply have to map these possible decisions to an XML DTD. Because XML uses a hierarchical organizational paradigm, it is straightforward to model any decision tree as an XML document. After creating the DTD, your developers have to write the code that takes the decision branches from its internal data structures and passes them to the XML parser so that it can construct the document.

You map the configuration decision tree to an XML document

DTD Source

The best source for XML-based BOM DTDs would be an industry standard. Such a standard could help avoid installation conflicts among different applications and magnify the effectiveness of management tools. However, a standard might be limited to a given operating system and certain class of application. Open Software Definition (OSD) is an initial attempt at using XML for software configuration.

Industry standards are emerging for BOMs

Document Life Cycle

The installation program creates documents and puts them on disk, where they remain until explicitly destroyed. Management tools and subsequent installation programs consume these documents. Comprehensive management tools may maintain a repository of all BOM files for a given set of machines. An installation program that installs an updated version of an application may destroy the previous version's BOM and replace it with a new one.

BOMs persist as long as the application versions they represent

Configuration and Logging Files

Business Challenge

Configuration files specify execution parameters

Many software developers use configuration files, so users or administrators can specify the application execution parameters declaratively. Such files are often referred to as "configuration files," "deployment descriptors," or "property sheets." For example, the file may describe the properties of a software component or even specify how to link multiple components together to form a particular application. A common problem in using configuration files is enabling third-party development tools to create them. For the development tool provider, a significant amount of work is often necessary to produce a properly formatted file.

Logging files record execution information

Software developers use logging files to track such information as usage, application statistics, and debugging data. A common problem in using logging files is enabling users or administrators to view them and third-party analysis tools to process them. A significant amount of work is often necessary to interpret the file format properly.

XML Benefit

XML delivers inter-operability

Using XML as the format for application input and output files makes it easier for everyone. By using off-the-shelf XML parsers, software developers avoid the low-level work of file manipulation. More important, XML DTDs make it possible to define file formats quickly and unambiguously. With access to the DTD, software development tool and analysis tool vendors can leverage off-the-shelf parsers to reduce the amount of work necessary to produce and interpret different file formats. Also, by defining an XSL stylesheet for input and output files, software developers make it easy for users and administrators to view the information in the files with their Web browsers. Sun's **Enterprise JavaBeans** standard uses an XML deployment descriptor to configure the transaction and security properties of server-side Java components. *Extensible Logging Format* (XLF) is an effort aimed at providing a standard for such logs.

Architecture

As shown in Figure 7-4, deployment tools create XML configuration documents and store them on disk. The application then reads them from the disk and uses the information they contain to control application execution. As the application generates appropriate data, it saves XML logging files to disk. Analysis tools or Web browsers then access the recorded information. Note that the same process is possible over a network instead of through the filesystem. Clients could download an input file that specified how to present a user interface. Distributed application nodes sending output files with logging information over the network to a centralized repository.

XML files mediate communication with external tools

Key Features

The distinguishing feature of XML configuration and logging files is that they are directly related to application execution. XML input files control application execution. XML output files contain the results of application execution.

The relationship to application execution is a key feature

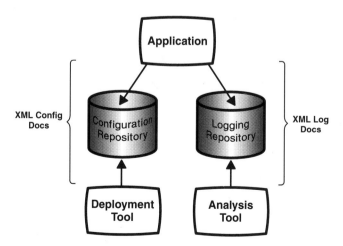

Figure 7-4: Using XML for configuration and logging

Development Process

You map application data structures to XML documents

For each type of file, you have to map the data types to an XML DTD. For configuration files, your developers have to write the code that will take the data extracted by the XML parser from input documents and put it into the appropriate internal data structures. For logging files, your developers have to write the code that takes the output data from its internal data structures and passes it to the XML parser so that it can construct output documents.

DTD Source

Convenience makes designing your own DTDs likely

In some cases, there may be standard DTDs. Some software component standards include DTDs that define the format for the configuration file. Certain types of output files such as transaction or security logs might also have standard DTDs. But because of the wide variety of possible configuration and logging files, as well as the ease of using XML for this purpose, you may design DTDs yourself.

Document Life Cycle

Configuration files may be persistent, logging files definitely are

Software development tools or even text editors create input documents and save them to disk. The application then consumes these input documents during application execution. Also during execution, the application creates output documents and saves them to disk. Analysis tools consume these output documents. Both input and output documents remain on disk until explicitly destroyed. Configuration and archiving tools may also maintain repositories of these documents.

Distributed Protocol

Business Challenge

Distributed applications often require custom protocols

Typically, the different nodes of a distributed application communicate using an application-level protocol running over standard networking protocols. Often, the nature of the application requires the use of a particular application-level protocol. For example, Web servers use HTTP. However, in some cases, nodes in a distributed application may need to exchange information unique to that particular application. An electronic commerce application may need to exchange information between the client and server to specify the contents of an order and authorize payment. Also, different nodes of a distributed application server may need to exchange hardware utilization statistics to perform effective load balancing. To provide for such exchange, vendors of such applications have to implement their own application-level protocols.

XML Benefit

A large part of implementing an application-level protocol is designing message formats and implementing the engine that will take data from internal data structures and put it in the appropriate message format. XML takes care of both these problems. XML elements and attributes already provide the basic model for indicating what information in a protocol message means. Software developers simply have to design a DTD for each particular message type. XML parsers take care of making sure that message instances have the appropriate format. Moreover, parsers extract the information in these messages and put it into internal data structures that the application logic can manipulate. By using XML, software developers gain enormous leverage in the design and development of application-level protocols.

XML serves as the protocol message format

Developers also get the benefits of XSL. Often, debugging distributed applications can be very difficult because it's hard to decipher the messages exchanged. When developing XML-based protocols, developers can simply specify an XSL stylesheet for each message type and they can view protocol messages in an easily readable format on any XML-capable Web browser.

Stylesheets are useful for debugging

Figure 7-5: The
XML-based dis-
tributed protocols
architecture

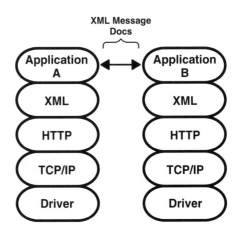

Architecture

*XML protocols run
on top of other
protocols*

As Figure 7-5 shows, the architecture of XML-based distributed
protocols is relatively simple. As with most application-level protocols, they probably leverage the standard TCP/IP networking protocols and the corresponding network drivers provided by operating
system vendors. They also allow developers to use HTTP as the message exchange protocol. HTTP engines are widely available and
most security firewalls provide options for **HTTP tunneling**, making it an attractive option. The XML parser sits on top of the message exchange protocol, acting as the message coder-decoder.
Finally, developers write their application so that it accesses the
information extracted by the XML parser, performs any necessary
processing, places the results in a data structure representing the
response, and instructs the parser to encode the response message
as an XML document.

Key Features

*The short life of
documents is a key
characteristic*

The key characteristic of an XML-based distributed protocol is that
remote messages exchanged over the network are formatted as
XML documents. These messages are extremely short lived.

Development Process

Implementing an application-level protocol requires first specifying
the allowable message flow. In operation, such a protocol consists
of messages flowing between two nodes in the distributed application. These messages must occur in a specific order—the nodes
must exchange handshake messages first, then exchange authenti-
cation messages, and so forth. After designing the message flow,
you must design the message formats. For XML-based protocols,
DTDs specify the format of different types of messages.

*You specify message
flow, then format*

With these elements in place, you must choose a lower level protocol for message exchange. They can exchange messages over raw
TCP/IP sockets or use a higher level protocol such as HTTP. Then
they must implement the control logic that governs the assembly,
sending, receiving, and disassembly of messages.

*TCP/IP and HTTP
are common XML
protocol transports*

DTD Source

For a given protocol, message types have a corresponding DTD.
In some cases, a protocol may be an industry standard and the
DTDs will be part of the standard. In other cases, the protocol may
be unique to a particular application and you will specify your
own DTDs.

*Custom protocols
require custom DTDs*

Document Life Cycle

The node sending a message in a distributed application creates the
corresponding document. The node receiving the message consumes the document, at which point the document would usually
be destroyed. An application could archive a complete or partial
transcript of protocol messages, preserving the corresponding documents. However, the large volume of such documents would typically make such an arrangement cumbersome except perhaps
during testing and debugging.

*Documents survive
only the transfer over
the network*

Glossary

Application programming interface (API)

A set of functions that an application or component exposes to external software. Programmers use an API to create software that accesses the functionality of an application or component.

Attribute

A piece of *metadata* attached to an element. See also *attribute specification*.

Attribute name

See *attribute specification*.

Attribute specification

An *attribute name* and corresponding *attribute value* in the start tag of an *element*.

Attribute value

See *attribute specification*.

Business object modeling

The process of representing business entities and business processes as objects, in the object-oriented programming sense, to facilitate the integration of different business application software.

CDATA

Abbreviation for character data. A string of alphanumeric characters that may not contain any white space characters.

COBOL

Abbreviation for Common Business Oriented Language. A computer programming language used in developing business application software, originally on mainframes.

Content model

The allowable type of content that an element may have. Possible content models include element content, data content, empty content, and mixed content.

Document element

The topmost *element* in an XML document's element hierarchy. All other elements within an XML document are part of a document element's content.

Document type definition (DTD)

A specification of the rules a group of XML documents must follow to be *valid* with respect to the particular DTD. Rules include the allowable types of elements, their content models, their attributes, and the allowable values of these attributes.

Element

The fundamental unit of content in an XML document. An element comprises the *element name, element content,* and any specified *attributes.*

Element content

The content associated with an element. It appears between the start tag and end tag of the element.

Element declaration

A statement in a *DTD* that declares an *element name* and a *content model* for the element.

Element name

The name associated with an element. In an XML document, it appears in both the start tag and end tag of the element.

Enterprise JavaBeans

A standard from Sun Microsystems that specifies a server application component model for Java.

Entity

An XML document structuring mechanism that specifies the substitution of an *entity name* with a fragment of content.

Entity name

See *entity.*

Extended link

In *XLink,* a link that has more than one target.

Extensible Stylesheet Language (XSL)

The W3C standard for describing presentation rules that apply to XML documents.

Extranet

A portion of the Internet used by an organization to foster communication with its suppliers, large customers, and strategic partners.

Float

A datatype declaration for floating point numbers in many software programming languages.

Formatting object tree

The hierarchy of format-specific elements created when an XSL processor applies a *stylesheet* to an XML document. This hierarchy is independent of any particular page rendering technology.

FTP

Abbreviation for File Transfer Protocol. A mechanism for uploading and downloading files between two computers connected by the Internet.

HTML

Abbreviation for Hypertext Markup Language. The language used to author Web pages.

HTTP

Abbreviation for HyperText Transfer Protocol. A mechanism for making requests and sending responses between two computers connected to the Internet. Commonly used for transferring HTML files from a Web server to a Web browser.

HTTP tunneling

The process of wrapping protocol messages in HTTP messages. Commonly used to allow the use of a protocol across a security firewall.

IDE

Abbreviation for Interactive Development Environment. A tool for developing software applications that includes visual tools such as browsers, inspectors, and probes.

Information engineering

The process of developing a comprehensive model of the information used within an organization to facilitate the integration of business application software.

Int

A datatype declaration for integers in many software programming languages.

Internet

The federation of interconnected public and private networks running the standard Internet Protocol. See also *TCP/IP.*

Intranet

A portion of the Internet used to connect systems within the confines of a particular organization and not accessible to outsiders.

JDBC

The standard Java programming API for accessing databases.

Link

In document markup languages, a piece of content that indicates the location of a related document or related documents and describes how an application should mediate access to that document.

Metadata

Literally, "data about data." Data used to indicate the role or meaning of other data. Database schemas and XML attributes are examples of metadata.

Namespace

The association of names in a distributed software system with unique segments to avoid *naming collisions.* For example, XML uses URIs such as "http://www.foocompany.com/names/acct-REV10" and Java uses the Internet domain name hierarchy such as "com.foocompany."

Namespace name

In XML, a URI that defines the unique segment for a namespace.

Namespace prefix

In XML, the prefix that appears before element and attribute names to indicate that they belong to the corresponding namespace.

Naming collision

In distributed software systems, where two software entities developed by different organizations use the same name. For example, the accounting department and fulfillment department of a company might both use the XML element name "status" for logically different elements.

ODBC

A standard programming API, developed by Microsoft, for accessing databases.

Parser

A software program that processes text, determines its logical meaning, and creates programming data structures to represent this meaning.

PCDATA

Abbreviation for parsed character data. A string of alphanumeric characters that may contain white space characters

PDF

Abbreviation for Portable Document Format. A standard format, developed by Adobe Systems, for representing documents in a platform-neutral manner.

Postscript

A standard format, developed by Adobe Systems, used to represent high-resolution page layouts.

Processing instruction

A part of an XML document's *prolog* that enables document authors to describe the processing requirements of the document to external software applications.

Prolog

The first part of an XML document that contains processing instructions and document type declarations.

Resource Definition Framework (RDF)

A W3C standard for defining the types of resources provided by an Internet application and how to access them.

Root element

See *document element.*

RTF

Abbreviation for rich text format. A standard format, developed by Microsoft, for exchanging documents between different applications.

SCSI

Abbreviation for Small Computer System Interface. A high-speed standard for connecting peripherals to computer systems.

Shared context

An agreement among multiple parties governing the format and interpretations of messages they plan to exchange in the future. In XML, DTDs and schema provide shared context.

Simple link

In *XLink,* a link that has only one target.

Skunkworks

A colloquial term used to identify unofficial or secret projects, usually performed by a small group of highly skilled engineers. Originally refers to the division of Lockheed that worked on top-secret U.S. military airplanes.

SMTP

Abbreviation for Simple Mail Transfer Protocol. An Internet proto-col for transferring electronic mail between mail servers.

SQL

Abbreviation for Structured Query Language. An ISO standard for querying relational database management systems.

String

A datatype declaration for strings of alphanumeric characters in many software programming languages.

Stylesheet

In XML and other structured document paradigms, a specification for which pieces of content to display, and the formatting with which to display them.

Tag

In a document markup language, a piece of *metadata* attached to an *element* that defines the boundaries of *element content*.

Tagged markup

The general approach of using *tags* to indicate metadata in a docu-ment. See also *tag*.

TCP/IP

Abbreviation for Transmission Control Protocol/Internet Protocol. A standard low-level protocol combination used for communica-tion in many networking applications.

Uniform resource identifier (URI)

The Internet standard for representing the type and logical location of networked resources. For example, the URI "http://www.foocompany.com/home.html" indicates the file path-name, domain name, and connection protocol for Foo Company's Web home page.

Valid
An XML document that is *well-formed* and conforms to the rules of a particular *DTD*.

Validating parser
A *parser* that verifies whether an XML document conforms to the rules of a particular *DTD*.

Well-formed
A property of an XML document that follows all of the XML syntax rules.

World Wide Web Consortium (W3C)
A cooperative industry organization that defines standards relevant to Web applications.

XML Linking Language (XLink)
The W3C specification that describes how to define links between XML documents.

XML Namespaces
The W3C specification that describes how to define *namespaces* in XML documents.

XML Pointer Language (XPointer)
The W3C specification that describes how to specify a particular element within a document as the target of a link.

XML Schema
The W3C specification that describes how to define the structure of XML documents and the datatypes used within documents with more specificity than DTDs.

XSL Transformations (XSLT)

The W3C specification that describes how to transform XML documents from one format to another. For example, using XSLT, developers could specify how to transform a document valid with respect to one DTD into a document valid with respect to a different DTD.

Index

Addison-Wesley Computer and Engineering Publishing Group

How to Interact with Us

1. Visit our Web site

http://www.awl.com/cseng

When you think you've read enough, there's always more content for you at Addison-Wesley's web site. Our web site contains a directory of complete product information including:

- Chapters
- Exclusive author interviews
- Links to authors' pages
- Tables of contents
- Source code

You can also discover what tradeshows and conferences Addison-Wesley will be attending, read what others are saying about our titles, and find out where and when you can meet our authors and have them sign your book.

2. Subscribe to Our Email Mailing Lists

Subscribe to our electronic mailing lists and be the first to know when new books are publishing. Here's how it works: Sign up for our electronic mailing at **http://www.awl.com/cseng/mailinglists.html**. Just select the subject areas that interest you and you will receive notification via email when we publish a book in that area.

3. Contact Us via Email

cepubprof@awl.com
Ask general questions about our books.
Sign up for our electronic mailing lists.
Submit corrections for our web site.

bexpress@awl.com
Request an Addison-Wesley catalog.
Get answers to questions regarding
your order or our products.

innovations@awl.com
Request a current Innovations Newsletter.

webmaster@awl.com
Send comments about our web site.

mary.obrien@awl.com
Submit a book proposal.
Send errata for an Addison-Wesley book.

cepubpublicity@awl.com
Request a review copy for a member of the media
interested in reviewing new Addison-Wesley titles.

We encourage you to patronize the many fine retailers who stock Addison-Wesley titles. Visit our online directory to find stores near you or visit our online store: **http://store.awl.com/** or call **800-824-7799**.

Addison Wesley Longman
Computer and Engineering Publishing Group
One Jacob Way, Reading, Massachusetts 01867 USA
TEL 781-944-3700 • FAX 781-942-3076